D1105933

LORD, WHO ARE YOU?

JORGE CARDINAL MEDINA ESTÉVEZ

LORD,
WHO ARE YOU?

The Names of Christ

Translated by Eladia Gomez-Posthill

IGNATIUS PRESS   SAN FRANCISCO

Original Spanish edition:
Señor, ¿quién eres tú?
© 1983, Año Santo de la Redención, Santiago

Cover art: *Baptism of Christ* (detail)
Andrea Pisano
From the South Door of the Baptistry
Florence, Italy
Copyright Timothy McCarthy / Art Resource, New York

Cover design by Roxanne Mei Lum

© 2004 Ignatius Press, San Francisco
All rights reserved.
ISBN 0–89870–957–1
Library of Congress control number 200303115834
Printed in the United States of America ∞

I dedicate this modest work to my brethren
who believe in Jesus Christ, the Son of God
made man in the most chaste womb of the Virgin Mary,
especially to those who work at
the Pontifical Catholic University of Chile,
as a humble tool to help them know our Savior,
in this Holy Year of Redemption,
proclaimed by our Holy Father, John Paul II,
to celebrate the 1,950 years since the Lord Jesus
died on the cross and gloriously rose from the dead.

JORGE MEDINA ESTÉVEZ, PRIEST
1983

CONTENTS

INTRODUCTION

In the year 1583 there appeared, in an edition printed in Salamanca, Spain, by Juan Fernández, one of the more famous works written by the renowned Augustinian friar Fray Luis de León (1528–1591): *On the Names of Christ*. This work has been widely acclaimed for the purity of its language, and it is rightly considered one of the finest examples of Spanish literature of the Golden Age. Literary critics, to their credit, have recognized its value and have analyzed its style and vocabulary. But it is a pity that the same attention has not been paid to the theological and biblical merits of *On the Names of Christ*, since Fray Luis intended in the first place to compose a work of theological and spiritual doctrine and not merely an exercise in classical Castilian rhetoric. The Augustinian scholar was especially fond of this work, written in his mature years, and it was well received by his contemporaries; this is demonstrated by the three editions, all printed in the university city (1583, 1585, and 1587), that appeared during the author's lifetime. In the second edition (1585), Fray Luis introduced important new material, and he prepared another, no less important, addition, which came to light only in the fourth edition (1595), after his death.

By "names" of Christ are meant certain words (in grammatical terms, nouns) that are used in Sacred Scripture to refer to Christ. One of them, "Jesus", is a name in the sense in which we commonly use this word today. The others, which are quite numerous and which are used with varying frequency, denote the nature or essence of Jesus, as, for example, "Son" or "Word", or some characteristic of his action, for instance, the fact that he is "Shepherd" or "Master". Sometimes one or another of these names does not designate Jesus exclusively, as is the case with "shepherd" and "son of God", although they are applied to him in a very special way. There are names, however, that apply only to Christ, such as "Lamb of God" and "Bread of Life".

At the end of the introduction to his book, Fray Luis explains

> the reason many names are given to Christ our Lord, to wit: it befits his greatness and excellence, the treasures of his most opulent perfection, together with the multitude of his ministries and of the other goods that spring from him and are poured out upon us. Just as they cannot be embraced with one glance of the soul, so even less can they be named with a single word. And as someone who is pouring water into a vase with a long and narrow neck pours it little by little and not all in a rush, so the Holy Spirit, who knows the limitations and narrowness of our understanding, does not present that magnificence to us all at once, but rather offers it to us bit by bit, as it were, telling us on one occasion some part of it under one name, and under another name some other part on other occasions. And thus the names that Sacred Scripture gives to Christ come to be almost innumerable, for it calls him Lion and Lamb, Door and Way, Shepherd, Priest, Sacrifice, Bridegroom, Vine, Shoot, King and Face of God, Rock, Morning Star and Orient, Father and Prince of Peace, Salvation and Life and Truth; and so on with countless other names.

Of these names, Fray Luis selected and explained only ten in the first three editions, adding an eleventh, which he did not live to publish and which appeared in the fourth edition.

The intention of this little book is not to summarize Fray Luis or to provide a commentary on his work. Its object is much more modest: simply to take up again the theme of the names of Christ for the purpose of drawing near to him with humility, in order to know who he is and what sort of blessings the Father imparts to us through him. The fruit of such reflection—or meditation, if you prefer—should be the *praise* of God for his love and for the wonders he has done and continues to do for us, *gratitude* for all his boundless gifts, and, as a consequence, *love* for him who loved us first. If some kind reader should find that he is becoming enthusiastic about this theme, which is old and yet ever new, I could recommend to him nothing better than to put aside and forget about these patchwork pages and to set about reading the incomparable classic by the master of Salamanca.

Before ending this brief introduction, I would like to point out that it does not seem possible to establish an entirely logical order for the names of Christ: one presupposes the other, and they are intertwined, like the flashes of a diamond pierced by the light at different angles. Nor should we think, because some of them appear only a few times, that they are less important. Thus the reader, as he becomes acquainted with this subject, will discover, little by little, a rich and limitless prospect for learning about Christ through the Scriptures: he will see "the unsearchable riches of Christ" (Eph 3:8) and in them find joy, peace, and a pattern of life.

Calleuque, Chile
February 1983

APOSTLE

*Brethren, . . . consider Jesus, the apostle and
high priest of our confession. . . .*

— HEBREWS 3:1

The word *apostle* appears only once in the New Testament as
a name for Christ. *Apostle* is a word of Greek origin that
means "one who is sent". In the Old Testament, God is
portrayed as sending the prophets, in particular (see, for
example, Is 6:8; 48:16; Jer 1:7; Ezek 2:3): "From the day that
your fathers came out of the land of Egypt to this day, I have
persistently sent all my servants the prophets to them, day
after day" (Jer 7:25). Thus, the name APOSTLE, which the
Letter to the Hebrews attributes to Jesus, is related to another
name of Christ, that of PROPHET. The last of those sent by
God before the coming of Christ was John the Baptist:
"Behold, I send my messenger [angel] to prepare the way
before me, and the Lord whom you seek will suddenly come
to his temple; the messenger of the covenant in whom you
delight" (Mal 3:1; Mk 1:2). "There was a man sent from God,
whose name was John" (Jn 1:6). And John himself would say:
"[H]e who sent me to baptize with water said to me . . ." (Jn
1:33), and: "I am not the Christ, but I have been sent before
him" (Jn 3:28). The mission of John the Baptist was to bear
"witness that this [Jesus] is the Son of God" (Jn 1:34).

Jesus presents himself as one who is sent by the Father. "He
who receives you [the apostles] receives me, and he who receives me receives him [the Father] who sent me" (Mt 10:40).

13

"I was sent only to the lost sheep of the house of Israel" (Mt 15:24), a passage in which the word "sent" has a meaning very close to that of SHEPHERD because of the reference to the sheep. Jesus says to Nicodemus: "God *sent*[1] the Son into the world, not to condemn the world, but that the world might be saved through him" (Jn 3:17), and "he whom God has *sent* [Jesus] utters the words of God" (Jn 3:34). Especially in the Gospel of Saint John, we find Jesus referring to himself repeatedly as the one sent by the Father (Jn 5:23, 30, 38; 6:38–39, 44, 57; 7:16, 18, 28–29, 33; 8:16, 18, 26, 29, 42; 9:4; 10:36; 11:42; 12:44–45, 49; 14:24, and so on). It is fitting to cite here those very clear words pronounced by Jesus at the Last Supper: "And this is eternal life, that they know thee the only true God, and Jesus Christ whom thou hast *sent*" (Jn 17:3). In the First Letter of Saint John, also, Jesus appears as the one sent by the Father (see 1 Jn 4:9–10, 14).

On one occasion, it is said that Jesus was sent by the Holy Spirit:

> [Jesus] came to Nazareth, where he had been brought up; and he went to the synagogue, as his custom was, on the sabbath day. And he stood up to read; and there was given to him the book of the prophet Isaiah. He opened the book and found the place where it was written, "The Spirit of the Lord is upon me, because he has anointed me to preach good news to the poor. He has *sent* me to proclaim release to the captives and recovering of sight to the blind, to set at liberty those who are oppressed, to proclaim the acceptable year of the Lord.". . . And he began to say to them, "Today this scripture has been fulfilled in your hearing" (Lk 4:16–19, 21).

This is one of those passages that sum up the mission of Jesus, and it is very dense. "To preach good news to the

---

[1] Cardinal Medina Estévez italicizes many words of Scripture to indicate his own emphasis. The reader may assume that any italics in Scripture citations are the author's.— ED.

poor" means to announce the good news of salvation to those who put their hope in the Lord alone. "Release to the captives" is, above all, deliverance from the power of Satan, that is to say, from sin and from the individual and social consequences of sin. "Recovering of sight" means not only the miracles performed on behalf of the physically blind, but also the gift of the knowledge of God and of the value of things in the light of faith. "Liberty for those who are oppressed" is something similar to "release to the captives". "The acceptable year of the Lord" evokes the forgiveness of debts and the reestablishment of the social order that took place during the Jewish "jubilee years" (see Lev 25 and 27; Num 36:4; Deut 15:1–18). Yet this text cannot be interpreted as though its meaning were exclusively social or political, because Jesus refused the temporal authority of a king (see Jn 6:15; 18:33–37; 19:12).

Jesus is the ONE SENT, or APOSTLE of the Father. No one, neither before him nor after his coming, is "sent" by the same title as he. However, as is the case with other names of Christ (for example, Shepherd, Pontiff, Master, Witness, Prophet), the name Apostle, too, is applied to men who, in turn, have been sent by Christ himself to continue his mission or, rather, to make his mission present at all times and in all places, under the ever-present influence of the Lord and of the Holy Spirit. There are some very significant passages in this regard:

> [Jesus] called to him his twelve disciples and gave them authority over unclean spirits, to cast them out, and to heal every disease and every infirmity. The names of the twelve apostles are these: first, Simon, who is called Peter, and Andrew his brother; James the son of Zebedee, and John his brother; Philip and Bartholomew; Thomas and Matthew the tax collector; James the son of Alphaeus, and Thaddaeus; Simon the Cananaean, and Judas Iscariot, who betrayed him. These twelve Jesus *sent* out . . . (Mt 10:1–5).

"[Jesus] went up on the mountain, and called to him those whom he desired; and they came to him. And he appointed twelve, to be with him, and *to be sent* out to preach and have authority to cast out demons" (Mk 3:13–15). To these Twelve Jesus himself gave the name or title of apostles, according to the Gospel of Saint Luke (Lk 6:13), although later others would receive this name as well (1 Cor 15:7), among whom Saint Paul stands out, who says of himself: "Paul an apostle— not from men nor [called] through man, but through Jesus Christ and God the Father" (Gal 1:1). The name "apostle" occurs almost eighty times in the New Testament, designating the disciples who have been sent by the Lord, with his authority; in about half of these instances the word *apostle* refers to Saint Paul, and that is why he is frequently called "the Apostle".

The mission of those sent by Christ is the same as his: " 'As the Father has *sent* me [Christ said to the twelve in an apparition after his Resurrection], even so I *send* you.' And when [Jesus] had said this, he breathed on them and said to them, 'Receive the Holy Spirit. If you forgive the sins of any, they are forgiven; if you retain the sins of any, they are retained' " (Jn 20:21b–23). It is clear that the mission of the apostles has as one of its more important objectives the forgiveness of sins, that is to say, to defeat the power of Satan. It is important to bear in mind that the mission of those sent by Jesus is sustained by the grace of the Holy Spirit; they do not go to proclaim their own wisdom or a human science but, rather, the gospel, which they have received as a deposit (1 Tim 6:20; 2 Tim 1:12–14) and of which they cannot dispose arbitrarily, but only as faithful stewards (1 Pet 4:10). For the same reason, just as no one can attribute the priesthood to himself, because only a man called by God can receive it (see Heb 5:5–6), in the same way no one can consider himself as having been sent unless he has received this mission. "And how can people preach unless they are sent?" (Rom 10:15). And because the first apostles received their mission from Christ himself, that same mission included the power or authority to associate with it other men who, in turn, would associate others, and so on until the end of the world, according to the testimony of Pope Saint Clement I (late first century). He who claims as his own a mission that he has not legitimately received is a false apostle and does not have within him the gift of the Holy Spirit. In the Church it is the Pope and the bishops who confer upon others the mission to proclaim Jesus Christ legitimately: they are the ones who have the power "to send".

BISHOP

You have now returned to the Shepherd and
Guardian[1] *of your souls.*

— I PETER 2:25

Only in this passage from Saint Peter is the name BISHOP applied to Jesus. This is a name of Greek origin meaning "watchman", "overseer", or "guardian", that is to say, it denotes the duty of being attentive to the needs of others and of protecting them from the dangers that lie in wait for them.

In the New Testament, the word *bishop* is used to designate those who are responsible for the Churches. In the Acts of the Apostles, Saint Paul addresses these words to the presbyters of the Church: "Take heed to yourselves and to all the flock, in which the Holy Spirit has made you *guardians*, to feed the church of the Lord which he [Jesus] obtained with his own blood" (Acts 20:28). It is necessary to point out that, in this passage, the office of guardian or bishop is found within the context of shepherding; it is related, therefore, to the name of "Shepherd", which belongs to Christ (and is the subject of another chapter). Saint Paul, writing to the Christians in the city of Philippi, mentions expressly the bishops and deacons who live in that community (Phil 1:1). The same Apostle is concerned with listing the qualities that someone in charge of the Church must possess:

---

[1] Greek, *episkopon*; Latin, *episcopum* = bishop.— TRANS.

18

This is why I left you in Crete [he says to his co-worker, Saint Titus], that you might amend what was defective, and appoint elders [*presbyteros*, priests] in every town as I directed you, if any man is blameless, the husband of one wife, and his children are believers and not open to the charge of being profligate or insubordinate. For a *bishop*, as God's steward, must be blameless; he must not be arrogant or quick-tempered or a drunkard or violent or greedy for gain, but hospitable, a lover of goodness, master of himself, upright, holy, and self-controlled; he must hold firm to the sure word as taught, so that he may be able to give instruction in sound doctrine and also to confute those who contradict it (Tit 1:5–9; see also 1 Tim 3:2–7).

While the episcopate is a heavy responsibility in the Church, it is understood that discharging this duty is required by pastoral charity. Perhaps this is why Saint Paul believes that it is a good thing to aspire to dedicate oneself to the service of others in the pastoral ministry (1 Tim 3:1).

The name BISHOP given to Christ suggests, in the first place, that those who have been called to be bishops of the Church must be conformed to Jesus. It suggests also that Christ, now glorious in heaven, is not unconcerned about us and his Church but, rather, watches over her with an abiding love: "Consequently he is able for all time to save those who draw near to God through him [Jesus], since he always lives to make intercession for them" (Heb 7:25). The ministers in the Church are but instruments of this saving action of Christ, which is ever real and ever present.

BREAD OF LIFE

"I am the Bread of Life."

— JOHN 6:35

Since ancient times, bread has been the symbol of all food: "In the sweat of your face you shall eat *bread*" (Gen 3:19) were God's words to Adam, proclaiming to him that, as a consequence of sin, work would be wearisome for him from then on. To "share your *bread* with the hungry" (Is 58:7) is equivalent to saying, "Give to the hungry something to eat."

In Moses' time, it was written: "And he [God] humbled you and let you hunger and fed you with manna, which you did not know, nor did your fathers know; that he might make you know that man does not live by *bread* alone, but that man lives by everything that proceeds out of the mouth of the LORD" (Deut 8:3). Although this passage seems to refer directly to natural, physical food, like bread, or to miraculous food, like manna, it contains a hint of a more spiritual meaning. When the devil tempted Jesus, he said to him: "If you are the Son of God, command these stones to become loaves of *bread*" (Mt 4:3; Lk 4:3); but Jesus replied: "Man shall not live by *bread* alone, but by every word that proceeds from the mouth of God" (Mt 4:4; Lk 4:4), citing the ancient words of the Book of Deuteronomy and giving them an explicitly spiritual meaning. "To live by the word of God" is an expression that signifies not only to know intellectually what God has said to us, but also to put it into practice, as Jesus explained: "I have food to eat of which you do not know. . . . My food is to do the will of him [the Father] who sent me, and to accomplish his work" (Jn 4:32, 34). This same meaning is apparent when Jesus says: "Blessed are those who hunger and thirst for righteousness; for they shall be satisfied" (Mt 5:6).

Just as in Deuteronomy and in Jesus' answers to the Tempter there is a transition from physical bread to spiritual food, which is the word of God, so too the mysterious multiplication of the loaves (Mt 14:13–23; Mk 6:30–46; Lk 9:10–17; Jn 6:1–13) provides Jesus with an excellent opportunity to speak of the Bread of Life (Jn 6:25–59).

The long discourse of Jesus that is recorded in the Gospel of John begins with the same theme of chapter 4:32–34: "Do not labor for the food which perishes [the loaves which had been multiplied], but for the food which endures to eternal life, which the Son of man will give to you. . . . This is the work of God, that you believe in him whom he has sent" (Jn 6:27, 29). These words serve to introduce the idea that Jesus is the Bread of heaven (v. 32–33), and, in the first place, for anyone who receives him with faith: "I am the *bread* of life; he who comes to me shall not hunger, and he who believes in me shall never thirst" (v. 35). This is why he reproaches the Jews for their lack of faith (v. 36). Food gives life and sustains it, so that when Jesus says that "he who believes has eternal life" (v. 47), he is summing up this first way in which he is the Bread of Life: through his life-giving Word. It is not a coincidence that in the same Gospel of Saint John, when the name of Word is given to Jesus, we read: ". . . [T]he Word was God. . . . In him was life, and the life was the light of men" (Jn 1:1, 4).

The same discourse presents a second meaning of this name, Bread of Life:

> I am the *bread of life.* Your fathers ate the manna in the wilderness, and they died. This is the *bread* which comes down from heaven, that a man may eat of it and not die. I am

the *living bread* which came down from heaven; if any one eats of this *bread*, he will live for ever; and the *bread* which I shall give for the life of the world is my flesh."

The Jews then disputed among themselves, saying, "How can this man give us his flesh to eat?" So Jesus said to them, "Truly, truly, I say to you, unless you eat the flesh of the Son of man and drink his blood, you have no life in you; he who eats my flesh and drinks my blood has eternal life, and I will raise him up at the last day. For my flesh is food indeed, and my blood is drink indeed. He who eats my flesh and drinks my blood abides in me, and I in him. As the living Father sent me, and I live because of the Father, so he who eats me will live because of me. This is the *bread* which came down from heaven, not such as the fathers ate and died; he who eats this *bread* will live for ever." This he [Jesus] said in the synagogue, as he taught at Capernaum (Jn 6:48–59).

This emphatic insistence on the words *eat* and *drink* made the Jews understand that Jesus was declaring something different from what he had said previously, when he spoke of his word as the food of faith. They understood that it was a matter of eating the flesh of Christ: "How can this man give us his flesh to eat?" (v. 53). Jesus did not correct himself, as though there had been a misunderstanding, but rather vigorously affirmed that it is necessary to eat his flesh and drink his blood, under pain of losing eternal life. This appeared intolerable to the Jews and also to many of his disciples, who after this no longer followed him (v. 66). It was then that Jesus asked the twelve apostles: " 'Do you also wish to go away?' Simon Peter answered him [on behalf of them all], 'Lord, to whom shall we go? You have the words of eternal life; and we have believed, and have come to know, that you are the Holy One of God' " (vv. 67–69). There remained a promise of Jesus, and the loyalty of his disciples, albeit in the darkness of faith, as expressed vigorously in the words of Saint Peter.

At the Last Supper, Jesus fulfilled the promise he had made immediately following the miracle of the multiplication of the loaves. The oldest account of the Last Supper was recorded by Saint Paul:

> For I [Paul] received from the Lord what I [in turn] also delivered to you, that the Lord Jesus on the night when he was betrayed took *bread*, and when he had given thanks [to God], he broke it, and said, "This is my body which is for you. Do this in remembrance of me." In the same way also the cup, after supper, saying, "This cup is the new covenant in my blood. Do this, as often as you drink it, in remembrance of me." For as often as you eat this *bread* and drink the cup, you proclaim the Lord's death until he comes. Whoever, therefore, eats the *bread* or drinks the cup of the Lord in an unworthy manner will be guilty of profaning the body and blood of the Lord. Let a man examine himself, and so eat of the *bread* and drink of the cup. For any one who eats and drinks without discerning the body [of the Lord] eats and drinks judgment upon himself (1 Cor 11:23–29; see also Mt 26:26–29; Mk 14:22–25; Lk 22:19–20).

By changing the bread into his Body and the wine into his Blood, Jesus brought to complete fulfillment his promise to give himself as the Bread of Life, and at the same time he solemnly gave to the Church the perpetual memorial of his sacrifice on the Cross, the new Passover and the seal of the New Covenant in his blood.

To receive with faith the body of Jesus in the Eucharist is to be fed with the true Bread of Life, so as to become more and more like him: "He who eats my flesh and drinks my blood abides in me, and I in him. . . . [H]e who eats me will live because of me" (Jn 6:56–57). And if every member of the body of Christ is identified with him, it follows that all of them together form one body: "The cup of blessing which we bless, is it not a participation in the blood of Christ? The *bread* which we break, is it not a participation in the body of Christ? Because there is one *bread* [Christ], we who are many are one body, for we all partake of the one *bread*" (1 Cor 10:16–17). Here we see how the Eucharist unites us to Christ, the Head of the Church, and to one another, since we are members of this body.

If Scripture says, in referring to the Jews who ate manna in the desert: "Yet he [God] commanded the skies above, and opened the doors of heaven; and he rained down upon them manna to eat, and gave them the grain of heaven. Man ate of the *bread* of the angels; he sent them food in abundance" (Ps 78:23–25), we can apply those prophetic words much more appropriately to Jesus Christ, as he himself did when the Jews said to him:

> "Our fathers ate the manna in the wilderness; as it is written, 'He gave them *bread* from heaven to eat.'" Jesus then said to them, "Truly, truly, I say to you, it was not Moses who gave you the *bread* from heaven; my Father gives you the *true bread from heaven*. For the *bread* of God is that which comes down from heaven [Christ], and gives life to the world" (Jn 6:31–33).

The name BREAD OF LIFE is related to the names WORD, LAMB, LIFE, HEAD, and MASTER.

BRIDEGROOM or SPOUSE

"Can the wedding guests mourn as long as
the bridegroom is with them? "

— MATTHEW 9:15

The image of the bridegroom and the bride, or husband and wife, serves in the Bible, from ancient times, to describe the loving relationship between God and his people. In the more ancient texts, the theme appears in the context of Israel's infidelities, especially an ongoing tendency to render worship to idols. God, Israel's Spouse, complains bitterly that his people take the selfsame gifts that he has given them and offer them to false gods. In order that the people might recognize their error, God sends them punishments, precisely because he wants to regain their love and seal with them in an everlasting covenant: "And I will *espouse* thee to me for ever: and I will *espouse* thee to me in justice, and judgment, and in mercy, and in commiserations. And I will *espouse* thee to me in faith: and thou shalt know that I am the Lord" (Hos [Osee] 2:19–20, Douay-Rheims). Later on, even though the central theme of Israel's unfaithfulness—her adultery with the gods of Canaan—has not disappeared, there is much insistence upon the gratuitous character of God's love for his people. Israel was chosen at Yahweh's initiative, without any merit on her part, and God expresses this in vigorous terms as follows:

> [A]s for your birth, on the day you were born your navel string was not cut, nor were you washed with water to cleanse you, nor rubbed with salt, nor swathed with bands.

No eye pitied you, to do any of these things to you out of compassion for you; but you were cast out on the open field, for you were abhorred, on the day that you were born. And when I passed by you, and saw you weltering in your blood, I said to you in your blood, "Live. . . ." And you grew up and became tall and arrived at full maidenhood. . . . When I passed by you again and looked upon you, behold, you were at the age for love. . . . I plighted my troth to you and entered into a covenant with you, says the Lord GOD. . . . I clothed you also with embroidered cloth and shod you with leather, I swathed you in fine linen and covered you with silk. And I decked you with ornaments . . . and a beautiful crown upon your head. . . . You grew exceedingly beautiful, and came to regal estate. And your renown went forth among the nations because of your beauty, for it was perfect through the splendor which I had bestowed upon you, says the Lord GOD. But you trusted in your beauty, and played the harlot because of your renown, and lavished your harlotries on any passerby. . . . You took your fair jewels of my gold and of my silver, which I had given you, and made for yourself images of men, and with them played the harlot [by adoring them]. . . . And you took your sons and your daughters, whom you had borne to me, and these you sacrificed [to the idols] to be devoured. . . . Behold, therefore, I stretched out my hand against you, . . . and delivered you to the greed of your enemies. . . . How lovesick is your heart, says the Lord GOD. . . . I will judge you as women who break wedlock and shed blood are judged, and bring upon you the blood of wrath and jealousy. . . . [T]hey shall stone you and cut you to pieces with their swords. And they shall burn your houses. . . . [Y]et I will remember my covenant with you in the days of your youth, and I will establish with you an everlasting covenant. . . . I will establish [renew] my covenant with you, and you shall know that I am the LORD, that you may remember and be confounded, and never open your mouth again because of your shame, when I forgive you all that you have done, says the Lord GOD (Ezek chap. 16, excerpts).

God is depicted as the magnificent king who takes in a poor abandoned girl and, when she has grown up, makes her his wife. Afterward the wife forgets that all that she has she owes to her husband: Israel forgets Yahweh and uses God's gifts to offend him by making idols for herself. God sends punishment so that Israel might reconsider, and finally, out of sheer mercy, he renews the initial marital covenant. Ultimately it shall come to pass that "as the *bridegroom* rejoices over the bride, so shall your God rejoice over you [Israel]" (Is 62:5).

The entire book of the Song of Solomon, the poetic summit of the Old Testament, can be understood in its deepest sense only if it is viewed through the prism of God's love for his people.

John the Baptist bore witness to Jesus, saying: "No one can receive anything except what is given him from heaven. You yourselves bear me witness, that I said, I am not the Christ, but I have been sent before him. He who has the bride is the *bridegroom*; the friend of the *bridegroom*, who stands and hears him, rejoices greatly at the *bridegroom's* voice; therefore this joy of mine is now full. He must increase, but I must decrease" (Jn 3:27–30). With these words the Baptist was expressing an outlook that is quite fair: the servant of Christ is not the owner of the Church; the fame of the servants is of no account; all that matters is the glory of the one Lord.

Jesus, too, made use of nuptial imagery. Indirectly, with reference to himself, in the parable of the ten virgins (see Mt 25:1–13), where he points out the need of being vigilant while awaiting the coming of the Lord and his judgment. Directly, in his response to John's disciples when they asked why his own disciples did not fast: "Can the *wedding* guests mourn as long as the *bridegroom* is with them? The days will come, when the *bridegroom* is taken away from them, and then they will fast" (Mt 9:15; see also Mk 2:19–20; Lk 5:34–35).

Thus Jesus gives himself the name of Bridegroom, and it is interesting to note that he does so in a context similar to the one used by John the Baptist.

Without explicitly using the name of Bridegroom or Spouse, Saint Paul applies the nuptial theme to Christ and the Church, precisely in order to emphasize the dignity of Christian marriage:

> [T]he husband is the head of the wife as Christ is the head of the church, his body, and is himself its Savior. As the church is subject to Christ, so let wives also be subject in everything to their husbands. Husbands, love your wives, as Christ loved the Church and gave himself up for her, that he might sanctify her, having cleansed her by the washing of water with the word, that he might present the Church to himself in splendor, without spot or wrinkle or any such thing, that she might be holy and without blemish. Even so husbands should love their wives as their own bodies. He who loves his wife loves himself. For no man ever hates his own flesh, but nourishes and cherishes it, as Christ does the Church, because we are members of his body. "For this reason a man shall leave his father and mother and be joined to his wife, and the two shall become one flesh" [Gen 2:24]. This mystery is a profound one, and I am saying that it refers to Christ and the Church (Eph 5:23–32).

In this passage the Apostle interweaves the metaphor "Head and body" with that of "Bridegroom and Bride" in such a way that, by saying that Christ is the Head of the Church, one also says that he is her Bridegroom, thus indicating what it is that he does for her: he loves her and gives himself up for her (v. 25), he sanctifies and purifies her by means of his Word and baptism (v. 26), he nourishes and protects her (v. 29). The fact that we Christians are incorporated as members of Christ suggests very strongly the depth of our union with him.

The Book of Revelation tells of the vision of heavenly glory: "And I saw the holy city, new Jerusalem, coming down out of heaven from God, prepared as a bride adorned for her *husband*" (Rev 21:2). Meanwhile, "The Spirit and the Bride say, 'Come.' And let him who hears say, 'Come'" (Rev 22:17), as if the pilgrim Church, prompted by the Holy Spirit, were expressing her yearning for Christ, her Lord, her King, and her Spouse.

The name of SPOUSE or BRIDEGROOM is related to that of HEAD, LORD, KING, LIFE. This name is a call to fidelity, to love, to homesickness for heavenly things, without implying any disregard for the temporal realities through which we journey on our pilgrimage toward the heavenly Jerusalem.

CHRIST or MESSIAH

He [Andrew] first found his brother Simon, and said to him,
*   "We have found the Messiah" (which means Christ).*

— JOHN 1:41

The name CHRIST, which appears around five hundred thirty times in the New Testament, is a word of Greek origin that means "anointed". It appears quite a few times in Sacred Scripture combined with the name of Jesus: Jesus Christ or Christ Jesus. From the name Christ comes the name "Christian". Furthermore, one of the oils used by the Church derives its name from Christ: sacred chrism.

In the Old Testament, an anointing with oil had a religious meaning: it signified an undeserved [*gratuita*] election by God, the consecration to a task, an office, or some use. Both persons and things were consecrated. Anointings were carried out with oil mixed with various rich perfumes (Ex 30:22–32).

Even prior to the covenant with Moses there are records of anointing as an act with religious significance: thus Jacob *poured oil* on the rock upon which he had slept when he had a vision of God in a dream (Gen 28:12–22): the rock was a sacred place (see Gen 31:13).

Several objects used in the worship of Israel were consecrated by means of an anointing with oil: "[T]he tent of meeting and the ark of the testimony, and the table and all its utensils, and the lampstand and its utensils, and the altar of incense, and the altar of burnt offering with all its utensils and the laver and its base; you shall *consecrate them*, that they may be most holy; whatever touches them will become holy" (Ex 30:26–29).

The Jewish priests were also consecrated by anointing: "And you shall anoint Aaron and his sons, and *consecrate* them, that they may serve me as priests" (Ex 30:30; see the description of the rite in Ex 29:1–37; Ps 133:2).

Some kings received an anointing, as well: Saul was anointed by the prophet Samuel (1 Sam 10:1), and he was called "*the anointed*", that is, "*christ*" (1 Sam 12:3); David, before becoming king, called Saul "the LORD's *anointed*" (1 Sam 24:6). David, too, was anointed by Samuel (1 Sam 16:1–13) and considered himself to be God's anointed (2 Sam 22:51; 23:1; Ps 89:20). King Solomon was anointed by the priest Zadok and the prophet Nathan (1 Kings 1:32–39). Cyrus, king of Persia, was called *the anointed*, not because he had been anointed with oil, but because he had liberated Israel (Is 45:1).

The prophet Elijah received from God the command to anoint Elisha so that he might be his successor as a prophet (1 Kings 19:15–21), although it is not clear whether the word "anointing" in this passage has a real or a symbolic meaning.

John the Baptist, that humble herald of the Savior, clearly stated that he was not the Messiah (Jn 1:20; 3:28), that is, the *Christ*.

The Psalms speak of the Messiah-king as the Anointed of God: "Your divine throne endures for ever and ever. Your royal scepter is a scepter of equity; you love righteousness and hate wickedness. Therefore God, your God, has *anointed* you with the oil of gladness above your fellows" (Ps 45:6–7). The prophets, also, employed this title: "The Spirit of the Lord GOD is upon me, because the LORD has *anointed* me to bring good tidings to the afflicted; he has sent me to bind up the brokenhearted, to proclaim liberty to the captives, and the opening of the prison to those who are bound" (Is 61:1); the angel Gabriel says to Daniel:

"Seventy weeks of years are decreed concerning your people and your holy city, to finish the transgression, to put an end to sin, and to atone for iniquity, to bring in everlasting righteousness, to seal both vision and prophet, and to *anoint* a most holy place [a Holy of holies]. Know therefore and understand that from the going forth of the word to restore and build Jerusalem to the coming of *an anointed one, a prince,* there shall be seven weeks. Then for sixty-two weeks it shall be built again with squares and moat, but in a troubled time. And after the sixty-two weeks, *an anointed one shall be cut off,* and shall have nothing" (Dan 9:24–26).

Jesus did not receive a physical anointing with oil to consecrate him to his mission. The anointings that he received in Bethany (Mt 26:6–13; Mk 14:3–9; Jn 12:1–8; Lk 7:36–50; Jn 11:2), the perfume with which Joseph of Arimathea prepared his dead body (Jn 19:38–40), and the ointments with which Mary Magdalene, Mary the mother of James, and Salome were planning to anoint him after his burial (Mk 16:1; Lk 24:1) were tokens of their respect and affection.

The Gospels give Jesus the name of Christ. At the beginning of Saint Matthew's Gospel we read: "The book of the genealogy of Jesus *Christ,* the son of David . . ." (1:1), and this genealogy concludes by stating: ". . . [A]nd Jacob [was] the father of Joseph the husband of Mary, of whom Jesus was born, who is called *Christ*" (1:16). Pilate knew that Jesus was being called the *Messiah* or the *Christ* (Mt 27:17, 22), and the Samaritan woman had heard of this name, for she said to Jesus: "I know that *Messiah* is coming (he who is called *Christ*); when he comes, he will show us all things" (Jn 4:25). Jesus' reply was short and solemn: "I who speak to you am he" (4:26). As soon as Jesus told Martha, Lazarus' sister: "I am the resurrection and the life; he who believes in me, though he die, yet shall he live. . . . Do you believe this?", she said to him, "Yes, Lord; I believe that you are the *Christ*, the Son of God, he who is coming into the world" (Jn 11:25–27). Jesus warned his followers against false *messiahs* and false prophets who "will arise and show great signs and wonders, so as to lead astray, if possible, even the elect" (Mt 24:24). Following the Resurrection, the Church very soon applied to Jesus the prophecies about the Anointed One. Thus Peter, speaking in Cornelius' house, says: "You know the word . . . which was proclaimed throughout all Judea, beginning from Galilee after the baptism which John preached: how God *anointed* Jesus of Nazareth with the Holy Spirit and with power; how he went about doing good and healing all that were oppressed by the devil, for God was with him" (Acts 10:36–38). Notice how these verses place a greater emphasis on the spiritual aspect of salvation than does the passage from Isaiah (Is 61:1), which is quite natural, all things considered. The Letter to the Hebrews, also, mentions the anointing of Jesus, citing Psalm 45:7 (Heb 1:8–9). In this, the first Christian generations were following the example of Jesus, who had applied to himself the prophecy in Isaiah 61:1 (see Lk 4:18).

The name of Christ or Anointed appears frequently in the New Testament in relation to the Son of God inasmuch as he has been sent to the world. One can say that the human nature of Jesus was anointed spiritually on account of its union with the Word of God, and the New Testament attributes this anointing to the Holy Spirit. *Messiah*, *Christ*, and *Anointed* are words that imply the consecration of the Son of God made man in order to bring about the reconciliation of mankind with God. If we recall that, in the Old Testament, priests, prophets, and kings were anointed, we can relate the name of CHRIST with the names of PRIEST or PONTIFF, PROPHET, and KING.

In the Church, anointing with sacred chrism is used in the sacrament of baptism, in confirmation, and in the ordination of bishops. It is also used in the consecration of chalices destined to contain the Blood of Christ and of altars on which the Holy Sacrifice of the Mass is celebrated. When the newly baptized are anointed with the chrism, we remember that baptism makes them members of Christ, who is Priest, Prophet, and King.

DOOR

"Truly, truly, I say to you, I am the door of the sheep."

— JOHN 10:7

The name DOOR, applied to Christ, appears only in the Gospel of Saint John, and in the context of the comparison of the Church with a sheepfold whose shepherd is Jesus (Jn 10:1–16). Curiously, in this same context Jesus gives himself two names, "door" and "shepherd", which are interconnected: "Truly, truly, I say to you, he who does not enter the sheepfold by the *door* but climbs in by another way, that man is a thief and a robber; but he who enters by the *door* is the *shepherd* of the sheep" (Jn 10:1–2). In this first passage, it would appear that the distinctive sign of the shepherd is precisely the fact that he goes through the door of the sheepfold. Perhaps the intention here is to put us on guard against false shepherds, those who make themselves known by the fact that they do not pass through Christ, who is the door. This is suggested by the explanation that Jesus himself gives his disciples, who had not understood the first comparison: "Truly, truly, I say to you, I am the *door* of the sheep. All who came before me are thieves and robbers; but the sheep did not heed them. I am the *door*; if any one enters by me, he will be saved, and will go in and out and find pasture" (Jn 10:7–9). Yet the comparison does not refer only to discerning the false shepherds but is aimed at showing that the only way to salvation is through Christ, as Saint Peter said later in the presence of the Jewish priests, the elders, and the scribes of

Jerusalem: "There is salvation in no one else, for there is no other name [besides that of Jesus] under heaven given among men by which we must be saved" (Acts 4:12). Even those who, through no fault of their own, do not know Christ can attain salvation only through him, although they are unaware of it.

The name DOOR is related to the Kingdom of God under the image of the House of God: "In my Father's house are many rooms" (Jn 14:2; Douay-Rheims: "many mansions"). The theme of the single DOOR is also related to the name of the sole MEDIATOR, and it is close to the name WAY. Its relation to the name SAVIOR is obvious.

HEAD

*[We] are to grow up in every way into him
who is the head, into Christ.*

— EPHESIANS 4:15

The word *head*, besides meaning the most noble part of the
human body, has a figurative sense that denotes the most
important part of a given thing, or the part from which
something begins. The word *capital* (as an adjective) comes
from *caput*, a Latin word that means "head". Expressions such
as "bridgehead", "head of the family", "head of state", "head-
quarters", "headwater", among others, have the connotation
of something outstanding or influential (see Is 7:8).

Jesus, in a veiled reference to himself, says to the Jews:
"Have you never read in the scriptures: 'The very stone
which the builders rejected has become the *head* of the
corner; this was the Lord's doing, and it is marvelous in our
eyes'?" (Mt 21:42; see also Mk 12:10; Lk 20:17). Jesus is
citing Psalm 118:22–23 here. Saint Peter, in reproaching the
members of the Jewish Sanhedrin for their rejection of Jesus
[Acts 4:11], refers to the same text; some translations—for
instance, the New American Bible—instead of the expression
"head of the corner", use the word "cornerstone". On the
other hand, in another passage, Saint Peter combines both
expressions, saying: "To you therefore who believe, he is
precious, but for those who do not believe, 'The very stone
which the builders rejected has become the *head* of the
corner,' and 'A stone that will make men stumble, a rock that

37

will make them fall'" (1 Pet 2:7–8), as in the Gospels. The underlying thought is that Christ is the foundation upon which the Church is built—a theme intimately connected with the name of ROCK. In all these passages, the word *head* is used in a rather figurative sense, having to do with the construction of an edifice.

Saint Paul developed the theme of the Church as the body of Christ, or a body in Christ, with the principal intention of emphasizing that Christians are the members of Christ united by the bonds of mutual charity; they are members who should respect one another in the orderly exercise of gifts that God grants to each one for the good of all (see Rom 12:3–11; 1 Cor 12:4–30). In this first development of the theme, Paul does not explicitly call Christ by the name of Head, but the idea is implicit in speaking about the body of Christ. This comparison of the relation of Christians to Christ with the relationship that exists between the members of a body is more profound than if he were speaking simply about a moral unity, such as the unity that exists among those who make up a society. This can be inferred from the argument Saint Paul uses to exhort the faithful to abandon fornication: "Do you not know that your bodies are members of Christ? Shall I therefore take the members of Christ and make them members of a prostitute? Never! Do you not know that he who joins himself to a prostitute becomes one body with her?" (1 Cor 6:15–16). Being incorporated into Christ is something so real that Saint Paul compares it, in its effects, with the physical relations of fornication: this union is much more than the moral and juridical bond that unites the members of a human community.

Later, when Saint Paul uses this comparison of the body of Christ, he speaks of him explicitly as Head of the Church: God the Father "has put all things under his [Christ's] feet and has made him the *head* over all things for the church,

which is his body, the fullness of him who fills all in all" (Eph
1:22–23). "[S]peaking the truth in love, we are to grow up in
every way into him who is the *head*, into Christ, from whom
the whole body, joined and knit together by every joint with
which it is supplied, when each part is working properly,
makes bodily growth and upbuilds itself in love" (Eph 4:15–
16). This latter passage goes further than the preceding one: it
affirms that Christ is the bond of unity in the Church and
that he continues to strengthen this union, so that charity
may be steadfast. Further on, in the same letter, the Apostle
says: "The husband is the head of the wife as Christ is the
head of the church, his body, and is himself its Savior" (Eph
5:23), adding that Christ feeds and protects the Church
"because we are members of his body" (v. 30). Here, the
analogy between the head–body correlation and the relationship between Christ and the Church acquires a special nuance, since Christ is presented as the Bridegroom of the
Church. The same theme appears again in another letter of
Saint Paul: "He is before all things, and in him all things hold
together. He is the *head* of the body, the church; he is the
beginning . . ." (Col 1:17–18); and somewhat further on Paul
says: "[Y]ou have come to fullness of life in him, who is the
head of all rule and authority" (Col 2:10), although, in this
last passage, the word "head" does not refer explicitly to the
Church but, rather, to the sovereignty over all creation that
belongs to Christ. In any case, "to come to fullness in him"
(v. 10) is the effect of baptism, as is evident in the verses
following (vv. 11 and 12), and baptism, in turn, applies the
fruits of redemption (vv. 13ff.) won for us through the Cross.

Just as other names of Christ are applied derivatively to the
ministers of the Church, so too we speak of the Pope and the
bishops as the visible heads of the universal Church and of
the local churches, respectively. It is obvious, however, that
neither the Pope nor the bishops are the source of the life and

unity of the Church; they are but ministers, servants, and instruments of the salvific and sanctifying action of Christ, who is the unique and ever-flowing source of grace. Saint Paul had to confront divisions in the Church of Corinth because of the excessive attachment of some Christians to certain ministers. They said, in fact, "I belong to Paul", "I belong to Apollos", "I belong to Cephas", or "I belong to Christ", and Paul replies, "Is Christ divided? Was Paul crucified for you? Or were you baptized in the name of Paul?" (1 Cor 1:12–13). Above and beyond the virtues and failings of the ministers, we Christians must look to Christ, the origin of all sanctifying power in his Church, whose sanctity is not sullied by the imperfections of men. Through the bishops, priests, and deacons, whose mission is precisely to make present and visible in the Church that characteristic of Christ the Head, we can become acquainted and come into contact with him who is truly the one Head of the body of the Church.

HIGH PRIEST or PONTIFF

"Thou art a priest for ever, after the order of Melchizedek."

— HEBREWS 5:6; PSALM 110:4

The theme of priesthood in the Old Testament is quite far-ranging: we read about Melchizedek (who was not an Israel-ite), *"priest* of God Most High" (Gen 14:18); about Moses' father-in-law, the *priest* of Midian (Ex 3:1); and, above all, about the *priesthood* of Israel, the origin and father of which was Aaron, Moses' brother, of the tribe of Levi (see Ex 28; 29; Lev 8; 9; 10; Num 4:1–49; 6:22–27; 8:5–26; 18:1–32; Deut 18:1–8, and many other passages). To that same priesthood, which was passed down from Aaron, belonged Zechariah, the father of Saint John the Baptist (Lk 1:5, 8). Jesus Christ, on the other hand, did not belong to the tribe of Levi or to the lineage of Aaron but, rather, to the tribe of Judah and the house of David (Mt 1:2, 6; Lk 1:27, 32, 69; 2:4–5; 3:31–33), and that is why his priesthood is not according to the order of Aaron.

The Jewish priesthood was in charge of divine worship among the people of Israel. This worship was centralized in one sanctuary, the Temple of Jerusalem, and was carried out principally through the offering of the various sorts of sacrifices prescribed in detail in the law of Moses. However, there are indications that Jewish priests must have had another ministry related to the word of God: "For the lips of a *priest* should guard knowledge, and men should seek instruction from his mouth, for he is the messenger of the LORD. . . . But you have turned aside from the way; you have caused many to stumble by your instruction; you have corrupted the covenant of Levi . . ." (Mal 2:7–8). At the time of Christ, the teaching of doctrine was, rather, the responsibility of the doctors of the law, who were not necessarily priests, and before that the word of God was entrusted especially to the prophets, who were not necessarily priests either, although Ezekiel (Ezek 1:3) and Jeremiah (Jer 1:1) were. It is interesting to read what the Gospel says about the Jewish high priest at that time:

> So the chief priests and the Pharisees gathered the council, and said, "What are we to do? For this man performs many signs. If we let him go on thus, every one will believe in him, and the Romans will come and destroy both our holy place and our nation." But one of them, Caiaphas, who was high priest that year, said to them, "You know nothing at all; you do not understand that it is expedient for you that one man should die for the people, and that the whole nation should not perish." He did not say this of his own accord, but being [the Jewish] *high priest* that year he *prophesied* that Jesus should die for the nation [of Israel], and not for the nation only, but to gather into one the children of God who are scattered abroad (Jn 11:47–52).

The evangelist sees in the words of Caiaphas a prophecy, the meaning of which he himself did not understand (Acts 3:17).

In general, the high-ranking Jewish priests were enemies of Jesus (see Mt 21:15–16, 23; 26:47, 57–66; 27:20, and others), but a group of Israelite priests did accept the Christian faith after the death and Resurrection of Christ: "[A]nd a great many of the [Jewish] *priests* were obedient to the faith" in Jerusalem (Acts 6:7). It is possible that it was to them that the Letter to the Hebrews was addressed—the New Testament book in which the teaching about the priesthood of Christ is developed at great length.

For every *high priest* chosen from among men is appointed to act on behalf of men in relation to God, to offer gifts and sacrifices for sins. He can deal gently with the ignorant and wayward, since he himself is beset with weakness. Because of this he is bound to offer sacrifice for his own sins as well as for those of the people. And one does not take the honor upon himself, but he is called by God, just as Aaron was. So also Christ did not exalt himself to be made a *high priest*, but was appointed by him [the Father] who said to him, "Thou art my Son, today I have begotten thee"; as he says also in another place, "Thou art a priest for ever, after the order of Melchizedek." In the days of his flesh, Jesus offered up prayers and supplications . . . he became the source of eternal salvation to all who obey him, being designated by God a *high priest* after the order of Melchizedek (Heb 5:1–10).

This passage summarizes several doctrines that are then explained in detail. Of course, it mentions as the principal duty of the priest the offering of sacrifices for his own sins and those of others. Then it states that no one can claim the priesthood for himself, because it is a gift from God. It goes on to say that the priesthood of Christ is according to the order of Melchizedek and not according to the order of Aaron. Finally, to the prayers and sufferings of Christ, that is, to his sacrifice, is attributed the salvation of those who believe in him.

The point of the statement that Christ is a priest according to the order of Melchizedek is to emphasize that his priesthood is *different from and superior to the Jewish priesthood.* Indeed, Abraham, the father of the Jewish priesthood, paid tithes to Melchizedek, thereby acknowledging him to be his own superior (Heb 7:2, 9–10); thus the tribe of Levi acknowledged in their father Abraham the superiority of the priesthood of Melchizedek. Moreover, "this Melchizedek, king of Salem, *priest* of the Most High God . . . is first, by translation of his name, king of righteousness, and then he is also king of Salem, that is, king of peace. He is without father or mother or genealogy, and has neither beginning of days nor end of life, but resembling the Son of God he continues a *priest* for ever" (Heb 7:1–3).

This is not to say that Melchizedek had no parents or that he was not born and did not die; rather, the author of the Letter to the Hebrews interprets the lack of these data (see Gen 14:18–20) as a prophetic sign of the eternal Pontiff, the Son of God made man. In Judaism, "the former *priests* were many in number, because they were prevented by death from continuing in office; but he [Jesus] holds his *priesthood* permanently, because he continues for ever. Consequently he is able for all time to save those who draw near to God through him, since he always lives to make intercession for them" (Heb 7:23–25).

The imperfect nature of the Levite priesthood meant that it could not bring to perfection the work of salvation, and so "another *priest* arises in the likeness of Melchizedek, who has become a priest, not according to a legal requirement concerning bodily descent but by the power of an indestructible life" (Heb 7:15–16). "He has no need, like those [Jewish] high priests, to offer sacrifices daily, first for his own sins and then for those of the people; he did this once for all when he offered up himself" (Heb 7:27). He did not have to offer sacrifice for himself, since our High Priest is "holy, blameless, unstained, separated from sinners" (Heb 7:26).

The Letter to the Hebrews insists several times that the sacrifice of Christ is unique: "[H]e entered *once* for all into the Holy Place" (Heb 9:12); "*Nor was it to offer himself repeatedly. . . . But as it is, he has appeared once for all*" (Heb 9:25–26); "so Christ, having been offered *once . . .*" (v. 27), "we have been sanctified through the offering of the body of Jesus Christ *once for all*" (Heb 10:10); "[having] offered for all time a single sacrifice for sins . . . , by *a single offering* he has perfected for all time those who are sanctified" (vv. 12, 14). This repeated insistence, as well as the statement that the priesthood of Christ remains for ever (Heb 7:20–28), has led many Protestants to deny that the Eucharist is a true sacrifice or that there are true priests in the Church. It is worth taking the trouble to examine these difficulties.

With respect to the Eucharist, the words of institution, as Saint Paul records them, show clearly that we are dealing here with a sacrifice: "This is my body which is for you. . . . This cup is the *new covenant in my blood*" (1 Cor 11:24–25). In reading these words we must not forget what is said in the Letter to the Hebrews:

> [T]he blood of Christ, who through the eternal Spirit offered himself without blemish to God, [shall] purify your conscience from dead works to serve the living God. Therefore [Jesus] is the mediator of a new covenant, so that those who are called may receive the promised eternal inheritance, since a death has occurred which redeems them from the transgressions under the first covenant (Heb 9:14–15).

If the New Covenant is in the blood of Christ, present in the Eucharist, and if Jesus himself commanded his apostles to celebrate the Eucharist, saying to them: ". . . 'Do this in remembrance of me.' . . . For as often as you eat this bread and drink the cup, you proclaim the Lord's death until he comes" (1 Cor 11:24–26), there can be no doubt that the celebration of the Holy Mass is a sacrifice. What must, indeed, be kept in mind is that the Eucharistic Sacrifice, celebrated every day by the Church, is not a *repetition of the death* of Christ, "For Christ . . . died for sins *once for all*, the righteous for the unrighteous, that he might bring us to God" (1 Pet 3:18), nor is it a sacrifice independent of the one carried out and consummated on the Cross and in the Resurrection. Nor does the Mass add more merit, as if the sacrifice

of the Cross were insufficient. Rather, in every Mass, the one
sacrifice of Christ is made present, and, through the celebration of the Mass, its salvific fruits are applied to us. Just as in
a great number of consecrated Hosts there are not many
Christs but, rather, his presence is multiplied, so too, in the
different Masses, *the sacrifice of Christ is not multiplied but, rather,
is made present in its perpetual reality as an offering and in the
communication of its fruits.* Thus it is clear that Catholic doctrine in no way declares the one sacrifice of Christ to be
insufficient; rather, it vigorously affirms its sufficiency. At the
same time, we believe that it was the will of Jesus himself to
entrust this one sacrifice to the Church, to which our Lord
gave the command and the power to perpetuate his sacramental presence.

Just as Protestantism has denied that the Eucharist is a sacrifice, for fear of attacking the sufficiency of redemption, for a
very similar reason it has denied that there are true priests in
the Church with special powers that are superior to those
of the faithful. Indeed, the idea that Israel is a "kingdom of
priests" (Ex 19:6) and that the Israelites "shall be called the
priests of the LORD, men shall speak of you as the ministers of
our God" (Is 61:6), was echoed in the New Testament:

> Like living stones be yourselves built into a spiritual house, to
> be a holy *priesthood*, to offer spiritual sacrifices acceptable to
> God through Jesus Christ. . . . You are a chosen race, a royal
> *priesthood*, a holy nation, God's own people, that you may
> declare the wonderful deeds of him who called you out of
> darkness into his marvelous light (1 Pet 2:5, 9).

> To him who loves us and has freed us from our sins by his
> blood and made us a kingdom, *priests* to his God and Father,
> to him be glory and dominion for ever and ever (Rev 1:5–6.)

> . . . [B]y thy blood [thou] didst ransom men for God from
> every tribe and tongue and people and nation, and hast made

them a kingdom and *priests* to our God, and they shall reign on earth (Rev 5:9–10).

In the mysterious context of the millennium, it is said: "Blessed and holy is he who shares in the first resurrection! Over such the second death has no power, but they shall be *priests* of God and of Christ, and they shall reign with him a thousand years" (Rev 20:6). These passages refer, with various nuances, to the *priestly status common to all disciples of Christ*, a quality that originates in baptism, which incorporates us into Christ, who is Priest, Prophet, and King, as it says in the formula for the anointing with the sacred chrism, which is performed immediately after the water is poured over the person being baptized. This common priesthood consists in the fact that "the hour is coming, and now is, when the true worshipers will worship the Father in spirit and truth, for such the Father seeks to worship him" (Jn 4:23). Saint Paul expresses this also, saying: "I appeal to you therefore, brethren, by the mercies of God, to present your bodies as a living sacrifice, holy and acceptable to God, which is your spiritual worship" (Rom 12:1), a worship that would have to include all nations, since the Apostle had been charged with preaching "the gospel of God, so that the offering of the Gentiles [= Christians converted from paganism, not from Judaism] may be acceptable, sanctified by the Holy Spirit" (Rom 15:16). Christian worship consists of the public liturgy of the Church, especially the celebration of the Eucharist and the other sacraments, and daily life in keeping with the demands of the faith. It is true that in the New Testament the word *priest* is not used to refer to the ministers of the Church; instead, this word and its derivatives are applied only to Jesus Christ and to the Christian people as a whole (see the terms used for ministers in Acts 15:2, 4, 6, 22; 20:17; Eph 4:11; 1 Tim 3:1–13; 5:17–22; Tit 1:5–9). The reason for this was the need to distinguish the Christian ministry from the Jewish and pagan priests; it would not have been so easy to avoid confusion if they had employed the same priestly vocabulary from the beginning. However, once Christian identity was assured and confusions eliminated, very soon, from the late first century, priestly terminology began to be used to designate the ministers of the Church, and that is how it continued without any arguments until the time of Luther (the sixteenth century). Since then, the Protestant communities do not use priestly terminology in referring to their ministers (nor do they accept, generally speaking, the sacrament of holy orders); the Catholic Church and the Orthodox Churches, on the other hand, in accordance with the ancient tradition, continue to use sacerdotal terminology to designate their ministers, without thereby causing confusion or a loss of Christian and Catholic identity. Protestantism fears that to acknowledge the priestly quality of the Church's ministers would be to obscure the unique and definitive role of Christ's priesthood and to create "classes" within the community. If these fears were justified, it would be a dangerous matter. A sound and correct Catholic theology cannot fail to emphasize that the priesthood of Christ is *absolutely unique*, that it is "eternal" in the sense that it is always present (whereas it is unorthodox to relegate its action to a historic past). No one in the Church is the "successor" of Christ. *There are "successors" of Peter and of the other apostles, but no one "succeeds" Christ*, for the simple reason that, in each sacramental act, the visible minister is no more than an *instrument* of the invisible High Priest, Jesus Christ. Saint Augustine expressed this in vigorous terms: "When Peter baptizes, Christ is the one who baptizes; when Paul baptizes, Christ is the one who baptizes; when Judas baptizes, Christ is the one who baptizes." The doctrine concerning Christ, the eternal High Priest, ought to be a source of humility for the ministers of the Church: what matters is not their own person or their individual qualities but Christ's action through them. The better the windowpane, the less you notice its presence, since it allows light to pass through it with perfect transparency. "This is how one should regard us, as servants of Christ and stewards of the mysteries of God. Moreover it is required of stewards that they be found trust-worthy" (1 Cor 4:1–2). There is no place in the Church for the *cult of the individual*: "He must increase," said John the Baptist, "but I must decrease" (Jn 3:30). For the faithful, this doctrine is an invitation not to pay inordinate attention to the human frailties of the Church's ministers. Those defects, sometimes quite real, unfortunately, do not prevent the saving grace of Christ from reaching us effectively through the sacramental acts, since it is he who baptizes, consecrates in the Eucharist, forgives sins, and so forth.

The name and ministry of Christ, as Priest and Pontiff [High Priest], is distinguished in an interesting way. This is the "name" to which a large part of the Letter to the Hebrews (chapters 3 to 10) is devoted, so that the New Testament dedicates a more elaborate and extensive theological reflection to this ministry than to any other. In order to appreciate the rich content of this name, a reading of the Letter to the Hebrews is indispensable.

The name of HIGH PRIEST or PONTIFF is related to the names MEDIATOR, APOSTLE, BISHOP, SHEPHERD, LAMB, and LIFE.

HOLY ONE or SAINT

*"The Holy Spirit will come upon you, and the power of the
Most High will overshadow you; therefore the child to be born
will be called Holy, the Son of God."*

— LUKE 1:35

The name HOLY ONE and the attribute of sanctity belong to
Yahweh: "Who is able to stand before the LORD, this holy
God?" is the question that the people of Beth-shemesh ask
themselves when they are struck by a plague (1 Sam 6:20).
This holiness of God is demonstrated already in the Old
Testament, in his mercy and forgiveness: "My compassion
grows warm and tender [says Yahweh]. I will not execute my
fierce anger . . . for I am God and not man, *the Holy One* in
your midst, and I will not come to destroy" (Hos 11:8–9).
The holiness of God is at an infinite distance from that of
men. "What is man, that he can be clean? Or he that is born
of a woman, that he can be righteous? Behold, God puts no
trust in his holy ones, and the heavens are not clean in his
sight; how much less one who is abominable and corrupt, a
man who drinks iniquity like water!" (Job 15:14–16). This is
why the Jewish high priest could enter only once a year, by
means of a special ritual of purification, into the holy place of
the tent of meeting (Lev 16:1–31), also called the "sanctuary"
(Lev 16:33). The sanctity of Yahweh is manifested in the
glory of his apparitions or theophanies. In the New Testament, there are many references to the holiness of God the
Father: Jesus himself calls him "Holy Father" (Jn 17:11); to

him the four mysterious living creatures cry out: "*Holy, holy, holy* is the Lord God Almighty, who was and is and is to come!" (Rev 4:8); *holy* is his name (Lk 1:49), his law (Rom 7:12), his covenant (Lk 1:72), his temple, which we are (1 Cor 3:17), and the heavenly Jerusalem (Rev 21:2).

Jesus is the Holy One because he is the Son of God, conceived by the power of the Holy Spirit (Mt 1:18, 20; Lk 1:35). At his baptism in the Jordan, he received the anointing of the Holy Spirit (Mt 3:16; Mk 1:10; Lk 3:22; Acts 10:38), and he was "full of the Holy Spirit" (Lk 4:1). Such is his holiness that, just as in the Old Testament the nearness of God aroused feelings of one's own unworthiness and impurity (Is 6:5), so too it happens with Jesus: "When Simon Peter saw [the miracle], he fell down at Jesus' knees, saying, 'Depart from me, for I am a sinful man, O Lord'" (Lk 5:8), a very natural reaction in the presence of him whom no one can "convict of sin" (Jn 8:46), "who knew no sin" (2 Cor 5:21), who "committed no sin" (1 Pet 2:22), who is absolutely "without sin" (Heb 4:15), and who, on the other hand, "loves us and has freed us from our sins by his blood" (Rev 1:5). When Jesus expels unclean spirits, they, upon recognizing in him the power and holiness of God, say to him: "Have you come to destroy us? I know who you are, the *Holy One of God*" (Mk 1:24); and "whenever the unclean spirits beheld him, they fell down before him and cried out, 'You are the Son of God'" (Mk 3:11), which suggests that the two names are identical. Peter, too, calls him by the names of "the Holy One of God" (Jn 6:69) and of "Christ, the Son of the living God" (Mt 16:16). So he is referred to also in the earliest preaching: "You [says Peter to the Jews] denied the *Holy* and Righteous One" (Acts 3:14), and the Father is invoked "through the name of thy *holy* servant, Jesus" (Acts 4:30). The risen Christ is described thus: "[These are the] words of the *holy one*, the true one, who has the key of David, who

opens and no one shall shut, who shuts and no one opens"
(Rev 3:7); and to him turn the souls of those who "had been
slain for the word of God and for the witness they had borne;
they cried out with a loud voice, 'O Sovereign Lord, *holy* and
true, how long before thou wilt judge and avenge our blood
. . . ?' " (Rev 6:9–10). The sanctity of Jesus is the same as that
of the Father: "*Holy* Father, keep them in thy name, which
thou hast given me, that *they may be one, even as we are one*" (Jn
17:11). Finally, Jesus' great prayer to the Father, on the eve of
his Passion and death, is: "*Sanctify them* [the disciples] in the
truth; thy word is truth. As thou didst send me into the
world, so I have sent them into the world. And for their sake
I *consecrate* myself, that they also may be consecrated in truth"
(Jn 17:17–19). Jesus goes forth to sanctify or to consecrate
himself by handing himself over to death on a cross, so that
his obedience might destroy the disobedience of Adam. That
obedience is the cause of our justification and salvation, and
for the same reason the inherent falsehood of sin is destroyed.
The death of Jesus reestablishes truth, that is, the acknowl-
edgment of the holiness of God, before whom we are sinners, and that truth brings us into the new life of children of
the Father. As a result of that work of salvation, Christians are
"*sanctified* in Christ Jesus, [and] called to be *saints*" (1 Cor
1:2), and are, to a certain extent, "*saints*" (Phil 1:1), since their
goal is to "be *perfect*, as your heavenly Father is *perfect*" (Mt
5:48), by the grace of God through which every disciple of
Christ can make his own the words of Saint Paul: "I can do
all things in him who strengthens me" (Phil 4:13), in such a
way that "no human being might boast in the presence of
God" (1 Cor 1:29) but, rather, like Mary, we might humbly
say: "My soul magnifies the Lord, and my spirit rejoices in
God my Savior, for he has regarded the low estate of his
handmaiden. . . . [F]or he who is mighty has done great
things for me, and *holy* is his name" (Lk 1:46–49).

The name HOLY ONE or SAINT is connected with the names of MASTER or TEACHER, MEDIATOR, LIFE, JESUS, HIGH PRIEST, and SON OF GOD, among others.

JESUS

"Joseph, son of David, do not fear to take Mary your wife,
for that which is conceived in her is of the Holy Spirit;
she will bear a son, and you shall call his name Jesus,
for he will save his people from their sins."

— MATTHEW 1:20–21

The name JESUS, which in Hebrew means SAVIOR, was well known in the Old Testament: the name "Joshua" has the same root (see the Book of Joshua; Hag 1:1; Zech 3:1), and the name "Jesus" itself appears several times (Prologue to Sirach; Sir 49:12; 50:27). The word also appears as a noun with the concrete meaning of "salvation" or "savior" (Hab 3:18; Sir 51:1).

In the New Testament, the name Jesus, as the proper name of the Son of God made man, appears no fewer than five hundred forty times, almost as many times as the name Christ, and frequently combined with it.

Just as the angel said to the shepherds: "I bring you good news of a great joy which will come to all the people; for to you is born this day in the city of David a *Savior*, who is Christ the Lord" (Lk 2:10–11), so too the risen Lord answers Saul, who asked him who he is, by saying: "I am Jesus, whom you are persecuting" (Acts 9:5). Saint Peter, summoned before the Sanhedrin, is interrogated by the Jewish high priests about the miracle he had performed the day before, when he cured a man who was lame from birth (Acts 3:1–12), and they ask him this question: "By what power or by what name did you do this?" His reply is solemn:

Then Peter, filled with the Holy Spirit, said to them, "Rulers of the people and elders, if we are being examined today concerning a good deed done to a cripple, by what means this man has been healed, be it known to you all, and to all the people of Israel, that by *the name of Jesus Christ of Nazareth*, whom you crucified, whom God raised from the dead, by him this man is standing before you well. This is the stone which was rejected by you builders, but which has become the head of the corner. And there is *salvation* in no one else, for there is no other name under heaven given among men by which we must be *saved*" (Acts 4:7–12).

Peter's statement is categorical: Jesus is the *only Savior*, just as he is the *only master* (Mt 23:8–10), the *only mediator* (1 Tim 2:5), the *only priest* of the New Covenant (Heb 7:24; 9:11ff.), the *only Lamb*, sacrificed once for all, who takes away the sin of the world (Jn 1:29; Heb 9:16–28), the *only judge* of the living and the dead (Acts 10:42).

This unique character of Christ as Savior does not prevent him from associating other men in his work of salvation, but it means that he and only he is and always will be its source and origin, not only in the past, but at every moment. Anyone who cooperates with him is his instrument but is neither his substitute nor an independent cause of salvation.

The word *salvation* is, no doubt, one of the key concepts in the Bible. It always has the sense of escaping, or being delivered from, danger, usually a very serious danger, frequently that of losing one's life. Sometimes, the terms *salvation* and *deliverance* are synonymous. In the Old Testament, salvation and deliverance often have a political connotation: the deliverance of Israel from the oppression of Egypt or from the Philistines or from other invading peoples or from those who were keeping them in exile. But, through these experiences of political liberation, Israel came to understand that her only salvation was in Yahweh: "O grant us help against the foe, for vain is the *help* of man!" (Ps 108:12). Occasionally, sin is viewed as the cause of Israel's political misfortunes, and the exhortation to repentance is accompanied by the promise of deliverance for the people from their oppressors (see, for example, Ezekiel, chapters 16 and following). "Look on my affliction and *deliver me*, for I do not forget thy law. . . . *Salvation* is far from the wicked, for they do not seek thy statutes" (Ps 118:153, 155). In the Book of Job it is evident that Job's faithfulness is rewarded with material prosperity, just as his detractors had seen, in his ruin, the punishment of his sins. We should keep in mind that in several languages the word *salvation* is identical to the word for *health* or *welfare*, that is, the same term can express the two distinct meanings. Yet we must not suppose that the sole concern in the Old Testament was with material or political prosperity: the Decalogue—that is, the Ten Commandments of the Law of God (see Ex 20 and Deut 5)—sets forth an ideal of justice and holiness that is valid in itself, even though disregard for it may bring on temporal calamities. Psalm 51, also, is a supreme expression of repentance, in which the focus is on God first, and only then on the punishment merited by sin.

The preoccupation with material prosperity and political liberation was found among Jesus' contemporaries and even among his disciples. The mother of the sons of Zebedee, James and John, said to Jesus: "Command that these two sons of mine may sit, one at your right hand and one at your left, in your kingdom" (Mt 20:21; Mk 10:37). In all probability, this was a rather worldly request, since Jesus responded by asking them whether they could drink from his chalice (meaning his sufferings, and not a cup at a banquet, as they understood it) and instilling in them the Christian rule that he who is the most important must be the servant of the rest (Mt 20:22–28; Mk 10:38–44). It is possible that a preoccupation of the same sort prompted Peter to ask Jesus what would be the reward of those who had left everything to follow him (Mt 19:27–30; Mk 10:28–31; Lk 18:28–30). Even after the death of Jesus, when he, having risen, encountered the disciples who were going to Emmaus, one of them said to him in despair: "But we had hoped that he [Jesus] was the one to *redeem* Israel [in the political sense; to rescue or liberate it]. Yes, and besides all this, it is now the third day since this happened . . ." (Lk 24:21). Perhaps it is because of this confusion between the broader, fuller, Christian meaning of salvation and the restricted sense that is usually given to the word *liberation*, emphasizing principally or solely its material and political aspects, that the Gospel and the New Testament avoid calling Christ by the name of "deliverer" or "liberator", although liberation, correctly understood in the fullest sense, is a concept not far from that of salvation. This confusion, which existed in Jesus' time, exists today as well; its influence can be observed in those Christians who put all the emphasis on so-called socio-economic structural changes and on "social sins", going so far as to assert that socialism is the Christian political ideal, without insisting too much (and sometimes not at all) on the conversion of the heart. Overlooked is the fact that the principal form of slavery oppressing man is that of sin, as well as the fact that the remaining forms proceed from human limitations (which are not always culpable).

By means of sin (Rom 5:12), death and perdition came into the world: "The whole world is in the power of the evil one" (1 Jn 5:19), so that the world is not in a state of welfare; rather, it needs salvation, which cannot come from the world itself. In other words, the world needs salvation, and that salvation can be granted to it only by God, through his Son Jesus Christ. This is how the Samaritans understood it when they said: "We have heard for ourselves, and we know that this is indeed the *Savior* of the world" (Jn 4:42), since "the Father has sent his Son as the *Savior* of the world" (1 Jn 4:14).

The meaning of the salvation Jesus brings is given in the angel's announcement: "He will *save* his people *from their sins*" (Mt 1:21). He "made purification for sins" (Heb 1:3) because "as it is, he has appeared once for all at the end of the age to put away sin by the sacrifice of himself" (Heb 9:26), so that he is *"the source of eternal salvation"* (Heb 5:9). When Jesus teaches us to pray, he teaches us to ask for salvation in its various aspects and especially in not falling into temptation and in being delivered from the power of the evil one (Mt 6:13). The one who has been set free from sin and has become a servant of God reaps the fruits of sanctification and, finally, eternal life (Rom 6:22).

Men's sinfulness, as well as their ignorance, gives rise to disorders in social life that are contrary to human dignity, to justice, and to charity. Every man has some responsibility, to a greater or lesser degree, according to his position and influence, in the work of correcting the things that are not in conformity with God's plan. Not to assume that responsibility is to be guilty of a sin of omission.

The name of JESUS or SAVIOR is more or less directly related to practically all the other names, since all the works of Christ are for our salvation.

KING

"You say that I am a king."

— JOHN 18:37

Since Jesus is, according to Sacred Scripture, the shoot or offspring of David (see Is 11:1), and since the angel at the Annunciation said to Mary that the child she was to conceive would receive from God "the throne of his father David, and he *will reign* over the house of Jacob for ever; and of his *kingdom* there will be no end" (Lk 1:32–33), it is clear that the name or title of KING belongs to him.

But this title of king, in Jesus' time, lent itself to many misunderstandings. The Jews could not forget that when their ancestors asked the prophet Samuel to give them a king such as other nations had, God took this request as a rejection of himself (1 Sam 8:7), as a desire on the part of the Israelites that he should no longer reign over them. And they could not forget that Samuel, speaking in God's behalf, predicted for them the abuses that wicked kings would commit against the people (1 Sam 8:9–18). It would seem that that petition contained an element of distrust with respect to God and of excessive confidence in men; they thought a human king would save them.

The history of the kings of Israel demonstrated that it was futile to place so much trust in men and that salvation could come only from a sincere search for God. Saul, the first king of Israel, did not please God (1 Sam 9:1—31:13). David, the second king (2 Sam 1:1—24:25; 1 Kings 1:1—2:12), was pleasing

59

in God's sight. He did commit a very grave sin of adultery and murder (2 Sam 11:1–27), but he repented and did penance after he was sternly rebuked in God's name by the prophet Nathan (2 Sam 12). Solomon, son of David (1 Kings 1:5—11:43), was a great king, known for his wisdom and for having built the Temple of Jerusalem (1 Kings 5:1–6, 13–38; 7:13—8:66). Unfortunately, he took foreign wives who led him astray and turned his heart toward false gods; his heart did not belong entirely to God, as David's heart had (1 Kings 11:4). At Solomon's death, his kingdom was divided, and the ten tribes of the north formed the kingdom of Israel, separating themselves from the two tribes of the south, which formed the kingdom of Judah. In each of these kingdoms there were kings, most of whom did not please God, because their religion was not pure, nor were their deeds just. Finally, both kingdoms were destroyed, and there was no longer a king in Israel. When the Maccabees rose in revolt in the third century before Christ (see the two books of the Maccabees), they did not claim the title of kings, but they were leaders of the people. When Jesus was born, Herod the Great reigned in Palestine; he was not Jewish but owed his power to the support of the Romans (Mt 2:5–12). During that era, Roman domination over the Jews started to make itself felt as more and more burdensome, and many of the Jews, even pious believers, hoped that the Messiah promised to Israel would be, first and foremost, someone sent by God to deliver them from Roman oppression (see, for example, Lk 24:21). That is how they interpreted the promises of the prophet Nathan to David (1 Chron 17:7–14). This misunderstanding of awaiting a Messiah who would be primarily a political figure came up again and again during Jesus' life. It was the fear of having in Jesus a political competitor that drove Herod to carry out the massacre of the innocent children in the areas surrounding Bethlehem (Mt 2:16–17). He thought that he could thus do away with the "king of the Jews", whose birth, announced to him by the wise men from the East (Mt 2:2), deeply disturbed him. When Jesus found Nathanael and told him he had seen him when he was beneath the fig tree, Nathanael answered: "Rabbi, you are the Son of God! You are the *King of Israel!*" (Jn 1:47–49). Probably Nathanael meant to say that he saw in Jesus the hoped-for Messiah, and it is quite probable that he, too, expected him to be a political liberator. The enthusiastic response of the Jews to the multiplication of the loaves led them to say: "This is indeed the prophet who is to come into the world" (Jn 6:14), but Jesus realized that they were not only acknowledging him as a prophet, but they also were preparing to make him *king*, and therefore he fled to the mountain (Jn 6:15). Thus Jesus showed that his mission was not political and that the public authorities had no reason to see in him a competitor or a revolutionary. This was made quite clear when they asked him whether or not it was permitted to pay taxes to the Roman emperor, and he replied: "Render therefore to Caesar the things that are Caesar's, and to God the things that are God's" (Mt 22:17–21; Mk 12:14–17; Lk 20:21–25). The entrance of Jesus into Jerusalem, to the acclamation of the people (Mt 21:1–10; Mk 11:1–10; Lk 19:29–40; Jn 12:12–19), recalled the passage from the prophet Zechariah that says: "Rejoice greatly, O daughter of Zion! Shout aloud, O daughter of Jerusalem! Lo, your *king* comes to you; triumphant and victorious is he, humble and riding on an ass, on a colt the foal of an ass" (Zech 9:9; see also Is 62). Soon after, Jesus again used the title of King to refer to himself in his description of the Last Judgment (Mt 25:34, 40). In that passage, several titles of Jesus are intermingled: "Son of Man" (v. 31), *"King"* (vv. 34 and 40), "Shepherd" (indirectly, in v. 32), "Lord" (vv. 37–44). The perspective of the Last Judgment indicates quite clearly the *otherworldly* sense in which the name of King is applied to Jesus.

The title "King of the Jews" played an important part

during the trial of Jesus before the Roman governor Pontius
Pilate. The four Gospels testify that Pilate asked Jesus whether
he was the *King of the Jews* (Mt 27:11; Mk 15:2; Lk 23:3; Jn
18:33), and they show, too, that Jesus responded in the affir-
mative. However, Jesus clarified what significance he attributed to his kingship:

> Pilate entered the praetorium again and called Jesus, and said
> to him, "Are you the King of the Jews?" Jesus answered, "Do
> you say this of your own accord, or did others say it to you
> about me?" Pilate answered, "Am I a Jew? Your own nation
> and the chief priests have handed you over to me; what have
> you done?" Jesus answered, "My kingship is not of this
> world; if my kingship were of this world, my servants would
> fight, that I might not be handed over to the Jews; but my
> kingship is not from the world." Pilate said to him, "So you
> are a king?" Jesus answered, "You say that I am a king. For
> this I was born, and for this I have come into the world, to
> bear witness to the truth. Every one who is of the truth hears
> my voice." Pilate said to him, "What is truth?" After he had
> said this, he went out to the Jews again, and told them, "I find
> no crime in him" (Jn 18:33–38).

There is no doubt that the Jews had accused Jesus of being a
political leader who threatened the authority of the Roman
emperor. That accusation was rather hypocritical, for those
same Jews wanted nothing other than to rid themselves of
Roman rule; only their hatred for Jesus could have led them
to accuse him, falsely, of something they themselves desired
with all their heart. In the sight of the Jews, Jesus was guilty
of having declared himself to be the Son of God (Mt 26:63–
66), but because they knew that that indictment would not be
accepted by Pilate, who was not interested in religious ques-
tions, they accused him of being a revolutionary. Pilate, in the
course of the interrogation cited above, became convinced
that this accusation was false, for Jesus told him plainly that his

kingdom was not of this world, and therefore Pilate did not
find Jesus guilty. When the Jews saw that Pilate knew they
had delivered Jesus up to him out of envy (Mk 15:10) and that
he was inclined to release Jesus (Lk 23:16; Jn 19:12), they
again insisted on their political accusation, shouting: "If you
release this man, you are not Caesar's friend; every one who
makes himself a *king* sets himself against Caesar" (Jn 19:12).
Pilate was frightened, and, although he knew that Jesus was
not a threat to the emperor, he feared that the Jews would
accuse him to his superiors and that such an accusation might
ruin his career. And so, with a hint of contempt, he said to
the Jews: " 'Behold your *king*!' They cried out, 'Away with
him, away with him, crucify him!' Pilate said to them, 'Shall
I crucify your *king*?' The chief priests answered, 'We have no
king but Caesar.' Then [Pilate] handed him over to them to be
crucified" (Jn 19:14–16). Once Jesus was condemned, the
soldiers made fun of him, clothing him in purple and crown-
ing him with thorns and putting a reed in his hand: all this
was a bitter mockery. As if that weren't enough, they knelt
down before him and struck him on the head, saying: "Hail,
King of the Jews" (Mt 27:27–30; Mk 15:15–20; Jn 19:1–3).
This ridicule was based on the assumption that Jesus had
attempted to be a king of this world, a political leader.

When Jesus was crucified, Pilate had an inscription placed
over the Cross, which read: "Jesus of Nazareth, *the King of
the Jews*" (Jn 19:19; Mt 27:37; Mk 15:26; Lk 23:38). It is
likely that Pilate wrote this inscription, not to ridicule Jesus
but, rather, to mock the Jews. That is how they understood
it, and they objected, asking him to change it to read: "This
man said: I am King of the Jews" (Jn 19:21). Pilate, however, did not change it, and with good reason. During the
crucifixion, the priests and Jewish leaders jeered at Jesus,
saying: "He is the *King of Israel*; let him come down now
from the cross, and we will believe in him" (Mt 27:42; see

also Mk 15:32; Lk 23:37); they all persisted in their fatal error of hoping for a political messiah, an earthly savior. That is why they did not comprehend the mission of Jesus, and they rejected him.

In bad faith, the Jews also accused Saint Paul of not observing the decrees of the Roman emperor by preaching that Jesus was king (Acts 17:7); yet it is quite clear from the circumstances described in the writings of the Apostle that he, a Roman citizen, respected the laws and institutions of the empire.

In the Book of Revelation, the title of "Lord of lords and *King of kings*" is given to Jesus (Rev 17:14; 19:11–16).

The title of King that Sacred Scripture gives Jesus is closely related to the "Kingdom of God", and he taught us to pray to the heavenly Father for its coming in the petition "thy kingdom come" (Mt 6:10). That kingdom is nothing other than the fulfillment of God's will, both in the personal sphere and in the social order, here on earth. Every disciple of Christ must do his part, wherever he is, so that the Kingdom of God may continue to grow among men in such a way that what we know by faith is applied to earthly realities and thus may prepare for what will be the definitive coming of the Kingdom of heaven.

It does not follow, from the fact that Jesus Christ is King, that the mission of the Church as such is to undertake the temporal government of nations, not even of Catholic countries, thereby replacing the political authorities. Yet it is her mission to proclaim the gospel and its consequences for personal and social life, denouncing when necessary what is incompatible with the teachings of Jesus and with the Kingdom of God. When the Church proclaims the gospel and its applications or denounces what is contrary to it, she is not identifying herself with any political position, nor is she acting out of an ambition to wield power. She is moved, rather, by the desire to serve God and mankind faithfully. If, in other eras, there were shepherds of the Church who, for various historical reasons, assumed the responsibilities of temporal princes, today such situations no longer exist, and the lessons learned from those experiments strongly suggest that they should not be repeated.

In ancient times, the royal dignity of Christ was expressed, especially in Byzantine icons, by representing him seated on the imperial throne, glorious, and clothed in purple, which was the color of the robes worn by the emperors. In those images, Christ's countenance reveals an infinite majesty, and sometimes the first and the last letters of the Greek alphabet—Alpha and Omega—are found on either side, indicating that he is the beginning and the end of all things.

In the liturgy of the Latin Church, the solemnity of Jesus Christ, King of the Universe, is celebrated on the last Sunday of the Church year. The opening prayer of the Mass for this feast expresses its significance:

> Almighty and merciful God, you break the power of evil and make all things new in your Son Jesus Christ, the King of the universe. May all in heaven and earth acclaim your glory and never cease to praise you.

The Preface to this Mass emphasizes that the Kingdom of God is "a kingdom of truth and life, a kingdom of holiness and grace, a kingdom of justice, love, and peace".

The name of KING is especially related to the names of SAVIOR, REDEEMER, and PRINCE OF PEACE.

LAMB

"Behold, the Lamb of God."

— JOHN 1:29

Lambs, together with calves, goats, and rams, were the animals used in the bloody sacrifices of the liturgy of the people of Israel. Sacrifices were acts of worship that consisted of killing an animal, shedding its blood, and burning all or some of its flesh upon the altar. When the animal was burned completely, the sacrifice was called a "holocaust"; when only part of it was burned, it was a peace offering, restoring communion, and the man who sacrificed the animal would receive part of it to eat with his family. The sacrifice was a symbolic act: the death of the animal and the shedding of its blood signified the will of the man who had offered it to offer his own life to God, thus acknowledging God as sovereign and Lord of all things, the only One to whom the tribute of adoration can be paid, the tribute that is expressed in a sacrifice. That is why, in Israel, it was always considered a very serious sin to offer sacrifices to creatures or to images of false gods. Throughout the Old Testament, and even before the law of Moses, there are descriptions of various sacrifices offered by men to God (see the Book of Leviticus, chapters 1 to 7).

Among the sacrifices offered to God, Abraham's stands out; in order to test him, God asked him to sacrifice his son, Isaac (Gen 22:1–19), although at the last moment an angel held back the hand of Abraham, and God provided him with a ram to be offered in place of the boy. The sacrifice of Isaac has always been considered a prophetic sign of the sacrifice of Christ upon the Cross. Very important also is the paschal sacrifice that was celebrated by the Jews on the night before their departure from Egypt (Ex 12:1–13): the blood of the lamb, which was used to mark the door posts of the houses of the Jews, freed from death the firstborn males of Israel, while the firstborn male children and beasts of the Egyptians perished. The Church has viewed this *paschal lamb* as an image of Christ, who by his blood frees us from sin and from everlasting death. The Jews received from God the command to celebrate the Passover each year (Ex 12:14, 24–27; Lev 23:5–8; Deut 16:1–8), and Jesus celebrated it, giving it a new meaning, instituting the new Paschal feast and the New Covenant in his blood in the celebration of the Eucharist at the Last Supper (Mt 26:17–28; Mk 14:12–25; Lk 22:7–22; Jn 13:1–2; 1 Cor 11:23–29). A prominent place in Israel was held as well by the sacrifice called the "continual burnt-offering", which consisted in the offering, each day, of two lambs, one in the morning and the other in the evening (Ex 29:38–46; Ezek 46:13–15).

Since the animal that was sacrificed ought to represent the purity of intention of the one who offered it, it was insisted that the animal be without physical blemish (see Ex 12:5; Lev 1:3, 10; 3:1; 5:15, 18). God rejected the sacrifices of sick or defective animals, signs of stinginess and of a lack of respect for the Lord (Mal 1:6–8; 1:13).

The prophet Malachi had proclaimed in the name of the Lord that "I have no pleasure in you . . ., and I will not accept an offering from your hand [that is, of the Israelites]," announcing that a time would come when "from the rising of the sun to its setting my name is great among the nations, and in every place incense is offered to my name, and a pure offering; for my name is great among the nations" (Mal

1:10–11). The Church has seen the fulfillment of this prophecy, and of the ritual of the perpetual burnt-offering as well, in the Eucharist or Holy Sacrifice of the Mass.

The most impressive passage in all the Old Testament referring to Christ as a lamb is in the poem about the Servant of Yahweh:

> Behold, my servant shall prosper,
>> he shall be exalted and lifted up,
>> and shall be very high.
>
> As many were astonished at him—
>> his appearance was so marred, beyond human semblance,
>> and his form beyond that of the sons of men—
>>> so shall he startle many nations;
>> kings shall shut their mouths because of him;
>
> for that which has not been told them they shall see,
>> and that which they have not heard they shall understand.
>
> Who has believed what we have heard?
>> And to whom has the arm of the LORD been revealed?
>
> For he grew up before him like a young plant,
>> and like a root out of dry ground;
>
> he had no form or comeliness that we should look at him,
>> and no beauty that we should desire him.
>
> He was despised and rejected by men;
>> a man of sorrows and acquainted with grief;
>
> and as one from whom men hide their faces
>> he was despised, and we esteemed him not.
>
> Surely he has borne our griefs
>> and carried our sorrows;
>
> yet we esteemed him stricken,
>> smitten by God, and afflicted.
>
> But he was wounded for our transgressions,
>> he was bruised for our iniquities;
>
> upon him was the chastisement that made us whole,
>> and with his stripes we are healed.
>
> All we like sheep have gone astray;
>> we have turned every one to his own way;

and the Lord has laid on him
   the iniquity of us all.
He was oppressed, and he was afflicted,
   yet he opened not his mouth;
like a *lamb* that is led to the slaughter,
   and like a sheep that before its shearers is dumb,
   so he opened not his mouth.
By oppression and judgment he was taken away;
   and as for his generation, who considered
that he was cut off out of the land of the living,
   stricken for the transgression of my people?
And they made his grave with the wicked
   and with a rich man in his death,
although he had done no violence,
   and there was no deceit in his mouth.
Yet it was the will of the Lord to bruise him;
   he has put him to grief;
when he makes himself an *offering* for sin,
   he shall see his offspring, he shall prolong his days;
the will of the Lord shall prosper in his hand;
   he shall see the fruit of the travail of his soul and be
      satisfied;
by his knowledge shall the Righteous One, my Servant,
   make many to be accounted righteous;
   and he shall bear their iniquities.
Therefore I will divide him a portion with the great,
   and he shall divide the spoil with the strong;
because he poured out his soul to death,
   and was numbered with the transgressors;
yet he bore the sin of many,
   and made intercession for the transgressors.
                              — Isaiah 52:13—53:12

It is true that the name "Lamb" appears only once in this text
(53:7), and that it is used there to indicate the meekness of the
suffering Servant, and not directly in the sacrificial sense, but
it is no less true that the phrase "when he makes himself an

offering for sin" (53:10) provides the key to understanding the whole passage. It is interesting to note that it was this passage about the suffering Servant that served as a basis for Philip's proclamation of the gospel to the eunuch of Queen Candace (Acts 8:32).

The First Letter of Saint Peter makes explicit mention of this name of Christ: "[C]onduct yourselves with fear throughout the time of your exile. You know that you were ransomed from the futile ways inherited from your fathers, not with perishable things such as silver or gold, but with the precious blood of Christ, like that of a lamb without blemish or spot" (1 Pet 1:17b–19). There is no doubt that Saint Peter attributes to Christ the name of "Lamb" because he sees in his death the great sacrifice of the New Covenant.

The name "Lamb", as applied to Christ, appears in the New Testament most frequently in the Book of Revelation: there it is used twenty-nine times, and it could very well be said that the proper name of Jesus Christ in the Book of Revelation is "the Lamb". The author speaks of the *glory* of the Lamb (5:6, 8, 12; 7:10; 17:14, etc.); the Lamb that *died* or *was slain* (5:12); the *blood* of the Lamb (7:14; 12:11; 22:14); the *marriage supper* of the Lamb (19:7, 9); the Lamb's *book of life* (13:8; 21:27); the Church, the *Bride* of the Lamb (21:9), and so forth. In each case, great emphasis is placed on the saving power of the blood of the immolated Lamb, that is, of Christ's sacrifice.

The name of LAMB is connected with the names of SHEP-HERD, SLAVE or SERVANT, and HIGH PRIEST or PONTIFF.

LIFE

"I am the Life."

— JOHN 14:6

The desire to live and to stay alive is a deeply-rooted desire in the human heart, and just as everything that is conducive to life makes a man happy, so, too, anything that threatens him with death saddens him. At the center of paradise, God planted the tree of life (Gen 2:9), and it was sin that caused the death of man (Gen 3:19; Rom 5:12ff.).

Scripture teaches us that there are two sorts of life: one that man possesses in a way similar to that of other living creatures and another that is lived according to God. In his nocturnal conversation with Nicodemus, Jesus said to him:

> "Truly, truly, I say to you, unless one is born anew, he cannot see the kingdom of God." Nicodemus said to him, "How can a man be born when he is old? Can he enter a second time into his mother's womb and be born?" Jesus answered, "Truly, truly, I say to you, unless one is born of water and the [Holy] Spirit, he cannot enter the kingdom of God. That which is born of the flesh is flesh, and that which is born of the Spirit is spirit" (Jn 3:3–6).

Natural life corresponds to natural birth, whereas the supernatural life received in baptism corresponds to being born of the Spirit. Saint Paul formulates the same teaching, saying:

> Do you not know that all of us who have been baptized into Christ Jesus were baptized into his death? . . . [S]o that as

Christ was raised from the dead by the glory of the Father, we too might walk in newness of *life*. . . . We know that our old self was crucified with him so that the sinful body might be destroyed, and we might no longer be enslaved to sin. . . . But if we have died with Christ, we believe that *we shall* also *live* with him. . . . So you also must consider yourselves dead to sin and *alive* to God in Christ Jesus (Rom 6:3–11).

It is Christ who saves us from the death caused by Adam in order to give us grace and eternal life.

If many died through one man's [Adam's] trespass, much more have the grace of God and the free gift in the grace of that one man Jesus Christ abounded for many. . . . Then as one man's trespass led to condemnation for all men, so one man's act of righteousness leads to acquittal and *life* for all men. . . . so that, as sin reigned in death, grace also might reign through righteousness to *eternal life* through Jesus Christ our Lord (Rom 5:15–21).

Jesus Christ himself affirms: "I came that they may have life and have it abundantly" (Jn 10:10), so that "where sin increased, grace abounded all the more" (Rom 5:20). Christ's work of giving life to those who were in "the shadow of death" (Is 9:2; Mt 4:16; Lk 1:79) is accomplished through obedience: "For as by one man's disobedience many were made sinners, so by one man's obedience many will be made righteous" (Rom 5:19), since Jesus "humbled himself and became obedient unto death, even death on a cross" (Phil 2:8), and "died for our sins in accordance with the scriptures" (1 Cor 15:3; see also Is 53:4ff.). The Resurrection of the Lord, of which Saint Paul says: "[I]f Christ has not been raised, then our preaching is in vain and your faith is in vain" (1 Cor 15:14), is the definitive sign of his triumph over sin, the wages of which is death (Rom 6:23). Thus, the death and Resurrection of Christ are the cause of new life for those who receive justification and grace from him. That new life, according to the spirit, extends even to the resurrection of the just, "For as by a man came death, by a man has come also the *resurrection* of the dead. For as in Adam all die, so also in Christ shall all be made *alive*" (1 Cor 15:21–22). In this way, the final resurrection will be the final triumph over sin: "The last enemy to be destroyed is death" (1 Cor 15:26), the wages of sin.

The Son of God made man, Jesus Christ, not only gives life, but he himself is *life* and *the fountain of life*, "for as the Father has *life* in himself, so *he has granted the Son also to have life in himself*" (Jn 5:26), and therefore "in him was *life*, and the *life* was the light of men" (Jn 1:4). Life is related to light, as death is related to darkness. That is why Jesus says: "[H]e who hears my word and believes him who sent me, has *eternal life*" (Jn 5:24), because to those who received him, "who believed in his name, he gave power to become children of God; who were born, not of blood nor of the will of the flesh nor of the will of man, but of God" (Jn 1:12–13). The great reproach that Saint Peter levels against the Jews is: "You denied the Holy and Righteous One, and asked for a murderer to be granted to you, and killed the *Author of life*, whom God [nevertheless] raised from the dead" (Acts 3:14–15).

Jesus is the Bread of Life (Jn 6:35, 40, 48ff.), not only because his "words . . . are spirit and life" (Jn 6:63), but also because his own eucharistic Body is life-giving food (Jn 6:53). As the Good Shepherd, he "lays down his life for the sheep" (Jn 10:11). To Martha, grieving over the death of her brother, Lazarus, he says: "I am the resurrection and *the life*; he who believes in me, though he die, yet *shall* he *live*, and whoever *lives* and believes in me shall never die" (Jn 11:25–26). But there is no entrance into this life, except through the knowledge of Jesus Christ: "This is eternal *life*, that they know thee the only true God, and Jesus Christ whom thou hast sent" (Jn 17:3). "He who has the Son *has life*; he who has not the Son of God *has not life*" (1 Jn 5:12). And, since love for Christ is inseparable from charity toward men, for "[as often] as you did it [= the works of mercy] to one of the least of these my brethren, you did it to me" (Mt 25:40), we also "know that we have passed out of death into *life*, because we love the brethren. He who does not love abides in death" (1 Jn 3:14).

Saint Paul summarized his attitude toward Christ in these words: "For to me to live is Christ, and to die is gain" (Phil 1:21), and therefore he could affirm that "*it is no longer I who live, but Christ who lives in me*; and the *life I now live* in the flesh *I live* by faith in the Son of God, who loved me and gave himself for me" (Gal 2:20).

The name of LIFE has an affinity with the names of VINE, SERVANT, LAMB, SAVIOR, LIGHT, HEAD, and BREAD OF LIFE.

LIGHT

Jesus spoke to them, saying, "I am the light of the world."

— JOHN 8:12

The name of LIGHT, applied to Christ, is peculiar to the Gospel of Saint John. "In him was life, and the life was the *light* of men. The *light* shines in the darkness, and the darkness has not overcome it. . . . The true *light* [Christ] that *enlightens* every man was coming into the world" (Jn 1:4–5, 9). Jesus says to Nicodemus: "And this is the judgment, that the *light* has come into the world, and men loved darkness rather than *light*, because their deeds were evil" (Jn 3:19). And to his disciples he says: "As long as I am in the world, I am the *light* of the world" (Jn 9:5). On another occasion, Jesus exclaimed: "I have come as *light* into the world, that whoever believes in me may not remain in darkness" (Jn 12:46). Saint Matthew's Gospel, quoting Isaiah 9:2, says: "The people who sat in darkness have seen a great *light*, and for those who sat in the region and shadow of death *light* has dawned" (Mt 4:16).

It is interesting to note that the reference to Christ as Light is frequently accompanied by the mention of darkness. Jesus says to his enemies in the garden on the Mount of Olives: "This is your hour, and the power of darkness" (Lk 22:53). Darkness is synonymous with the work of Satan, who is lies and confusion; at the moment Jesus appears to Saul, he says that he will send Saul to the Gentiles, "to open their eyes, that they may turn from darkness to *light* and from the power of Satan to God, that they may receive forgiveness of sins and

75

a place among those who are sanctified by faith in me" (Acts 26:18). To turn from darkness to light is to turn from sin to Christ: "For every one who does evil hates the *light*, and does not come to the *light*, lest his deeds should be exposed. But he who does what is true comes to the *light*, that it may be clearly seen that his deeds have been wrought in God" (Jn 3:20–21).

Jesus communicates his light to his disciples: "[B]elieve in the *light*, that you may become sons of *light*" (Jn 12:36).

> Once you were darkness, but now you are *light* in the Lord; walk as children of *light* (for the fruit of *light* is found in all that is good and right and true), and try to learn what is pleasing to the Lord. Take no part in the unfruitful works of darkness . . . for anything that becomes visible is *light*. Therefore it is said, "Awake, O sleeper, and arise from the dead, and Christ *shall give you light*" (Eph 5:8–10, 13–14).

Once a disciple has received, by faith, the light of Christ, he has the obligation to communicate it to others.

> "*You are the light of the world.* A city set on a hill cannot be hid. Nor do men light a lamp and put it under a bushel, but on a stand, and it gives light to all in the house. Let your *light* so shine before men, that they may see your good works and give glory to your Father who is in heaven" (Mt 5:14–16).

LIGHT, as a name of Christ, is related to the titles of MASTER, WORD, PROPHET, WITNESS, and DAWN [ORIENT]. This last name appears only once, in Luke 1:76–80:

> And you, child, will be called the prophet of the Most High; for you [John the Baptist] will go before the Lord to prepare his ways, to give knowledge of salvation to his people in the forgiveness of their sins, through the tender mercy of our God, when *the day shall dawn* upon us from on high to *give light* to those who sit in darkness and in the shadow of death, to guide our feet into the way of peace.

The idea that the disciple of Christ is a son of light and is illuminated by him means that he has been called to know God and his plan of salvation, which is the source of confidence and gladness. It means also that the life of the Christian must be marked by truth, candor, simplicity, uprightness, and sincerity.

LORD

Thomas answered him: "My Lord and My God!"

— JOHN 20:28

In ancient times, there was a notion that the "gods" were territorial: every place had its own "god", whose power was limited to one particular city or region. Yahweh, on the contrary, is not only the God of Israel; he is, rather, the "God of gods and *Lord of lords*" (Deut 10:17). "O give thanks to the God of gods, for his steadfast love endures for ever. O give thanks to the *Lord of lords*, for his steadfast love endures for ever" (Ps 136:2–3). For this reason, Moses says to the people of Israel: "Behold, to the LORD your God belong heaven and the heaven of heavens, the earth with all that is in it" (Deut 10:14). This universal dominion of Yahweh is the reason why he alone, and no emperor, is entitled in all truth and justice to the name "Lord of lords", because he alone is the Lord of all the earth: "Behold, the ark of the covenant of the *Lord of all the earth* [Yahweh] is to pass over before you into the Jordan" (Josh 3:11). "You . . . shall devote their gain [spoils] to the LORD, their wealth to the *Lord of the whole earth*" (Mic 4:13); "The mountains melt like wax before the LORD, before the *Lord of all the earth*" (Ps 97:5). Israel, imbued with a profound reverence for the sacred name of God, Yahweh, and filled with a holy fear of him, joined that name to the name "Adonai", that is, "my Lord", an expression of trust that, at the same time, acknowledges the absolute dominion of God. "O Lord GOD, forgive!" (Amos 7:2); " 'O Lord GOD, destroy

78

not thy people'" (Deut 9:26); "O LORD, my Lord, my strong deliverer" (Ps 140:7). Later on, the Israelites no longer dared pronounce the ineffable name of Yahweh, and they simply called him Lord or gave him other titles. "Praise the Lord for he is *good*" [see Ps 136:1]; "Praise the Lord, *Israel's shield*" [see Ps 136:12–16]; "Praise the *Creator of the universe*" [see Ps 136:5–9]; "Praise the *deliverer of Israel*" [see Ps 136:10–11]; "Praise the *builder of his city* and of his sanctuary" [see Heb 11:10; Ex 36–38]; "Praise the *Mighty One of Jacob*" [see Is 60:16]; "Praise *him who chose Zion*" [see Ps 78:68]; "Praise *the King over great kings*" [see Ps 136:17–20]. By then every Israelite knew that to speak about the Lord was a way of mentioning God and that LORD was a divine name.

In the Gospels, the name of Lord is sometimes given to Jesus: "And when the *Lord* saw her [the widow] he had compassion on her" (Lk 7:13); "She [Martha] had a sister called Mary, who sat at the *Lord's* feet and listened to his teaching" (Lk 10:39; see v. 41); "It was Mary who anointed the *Lord* with ointment. . . . So the sisters sent to him [Jesus], saying, '*Lord*, he whom you love is ill'" (Jn 11:2–3). Jesus, in disputing with the Pharisees, makes them see that David calls the Messiah *"my Lord"*, even though the Messiah is to be the descendant of David (Mt 22:43–45; Mk 12:35–37; Lk 20:42–44); in this way Jesus suggests, at least implicitly, that the name Lord belongs to him. Elizabeth had attributed this title to him before his birth, when she greeted Mary, saying: "Blessed are you among women, and blessed is the fruit of your womb! And why is this granted me, that the mother of my *Lord* should come to me?" (Lk 1:42–43); so did the angel who announced his birth to the shepherds: "To you is born this day in the city of David a Savior, who is Christ the *Lord*" (Lk 2:11).

The early Church acknowledged the Lord Jesus to be the son of David, as Saint Peter testifies: "David . . . says, 'The

Lord said to my *Lord*, Sit at my right hand, till I make thy enemies a stool for thy feet.' Let all the house of Israel therefore know assuredly that God [the Father] has made him both *Lord* and Christ, this Jesus whom you crucified" (Acts 2:34–36). In the earliest profession of faith, the affirmation that "Jesus is Lord" played a very important role (Rom 10:9; 1 Cor 12:3; Col 2:6); and, in the ancient prayers of the liturgy, the Aramaic formula "Marana tha!", which means "Come, Lord Jesus", is repeated with longing and hope (1 Cor 16:22; Rev 22:20). The meaning of the word "Lord", when applied to Jesus, is so strong that Peter says in Cornelius' house: ". . . God shows no partiality, but in every nation any one who fears him and does what is right is acceptable to him. You know the word which he sent to Israel, preaching good news of peace by Jesus Christ; he is *Lord* of all" (Acts 10:34–36); this last title, until then, had been reserved for Yahweh. Saint Paul vigorously affirms the same thing: "God has highly exalted him and bestowed on him the name which is above every name, that at the name of Jesus every knee should bow, in heaven and on earth and under the earth, and every tongue confess that Jesus Christ is *Lord*, to the glory of God the Father" (Phil 2:9–11). The kings of the earth "will make war on the Lamb, and the Lamb will conquer them, for he is *Lord of lords* and King of kings" (Rev 17:14); that Lamb is the Word of God who "on his robe and on his thigh . . . has a name inscribed, King of kings and *Lord of lords*" (Rev 19:16), a name proper to God the Father, as another Pauline passage testifies:

> In the presence of God who gives life to all things, and of Christ Jesus who in his testimony before Pontius Pilate made the good confession, I charge you to keep the commandment unstained and free from reproach until the appearing of our *Lord* Jesus Christ; and this will be made manifest at the proper time by the blessed and only Sovereign, the King of kings and

Lord of lords, who alone has immortality and dwells in unapproachable light, whom no man has ever seen or can see. To him be honor and eternal dominion. Amen (1 Tim 6:13–16).

It is Jesus who gives meaning to Christian life:

He also who eats, eats in honor of the *Lord*, since he gives thanks to God; while he who abstains, abstains in honor of the *Lord* and gives thanks to God. None of us lives to himself, and none of us dies to himself. If we live, we live to the *Lord*, and if we die, we die to the *Lord*; so then, whether we live or whether we die, we are the *Lord's*. For to this end Christ died and lived again, that he might be *Lord* both of the dead and of the living (Rom 14:6b–9).

In this sense, then, the name "Lord" means the center or reference point: "And whatever you do, in word or deed, do everything in the name of the *Lord* Jesus, giving thanks to God the Father through him" (Col 3:17). All of this extremely rich religious meaning of the name "Lord" necessarily clashed with the pagan custom of attributing this title to the Roman emperor (see Acts 25:26).

In the New Testament, the name of LORD is applied most often to Jesus and to him especially, as we have seen, after he rose from the dead. The transfer of this divine name to Christ is a sign of his divinity. In the liturgical prayers of the Church, the name "Lord" designates both the Father and the incarnate Son of God, so that sometimes only the context allows us to determine of whom or to whom the prayer is speaking by means of this title. Only once, in the Nicene Creed, is this name given to the Holy Spirit, who is called "the Lord and giver of life".

As used in Christian devotions, the name "Lord" has an endearing connotation, an especially loving tone. This can be perceived in the words of the apostle Thomas, who, reproached for his incredulity, addresses Jesus as follows: "My

Lord and my God" (Jn 20:28). This same affectionate quality is felt in the exclamation of John—the disciple whom Jesus loved (Jn 21:7) and the only apostle who had accompanied him to the foot of the Cross (Jn 19:26–27)—when he saw the miraculous number of fish that they had had by following the instructions of the Risen One, whom they had not recognized at first, on the shore of the Sea of Galilee: "It is the Lord!" (Jn 21:7; see also Jn 21:20–21 and Mt 26:22).

The name of LORD is related to the titles of KING, SON OF GOD, SON OF MAN, and SERVANT.

MASTER or TEACHER

"You call me Teacher and Lord; and you are right, for so I am."

— JOHN 13:13

At least forty-five times the name of MASTER [or TEACHER] is given to Jesus in the holy Gospels. Many times it is the title with which people address him when they ask him a question: "Good *Teacher*, what shall I do to inherit eternal life?" (Lk 18:18; Mt 19:16; Mk 10:17). On other occasions, the adversaries of Jesus, speaking to his disciples, refer to him as "your *Teacher*" (Mt 9:11) or "your *Master*" (Mk 2:16, Douay-Rheims), as though insinuating that they do not acknowledge him as such. In fact, when the Jewish chief priests and the Pharisees asked Pilate for a guard to watch over Jesus' tomb, they said to him: "Sir, we remember how that impostor said, while he was still alive, 'After three days I will rise again'" (Mt 27:63).

The title of "master" or "teacher" was well-known in Israel: Jesus says to Nicodemus: "You are a teacher of Israel" (see Jn 3:10). Nicodemus calls Jesus "*Rabbi*" (Jn 3:2), but, even before that, two disciples of John the Baptist had addressed him by the same title: "'*Rabbi*' (which means *Teacher*), 'where are you staying?'" (Jn 1:38). Perhaps these disciples of John, having witnessed the reverence that the Baptist showed Jesus, called him "teacher" as an initial sign that they would be his followers. With this encounter, Jesus began to call his first disciples. The word "master", which appears already at the beginning of the Gospel of Saint John as a title of Jesus, also appears at the conclusion, spoken by Mary Magdalene. When Jesus appears to her near the tomb after his Resurrection, she, upon recognizing him, says to him: "'Rab-boni!' (which means *Teacher*)." Actually, "Rabboni", literally translated, is "my Master".

But Jesus was not just one master among many. He himself uses the word as a proper name. When he sends his disciples to prepare the Passover meal, to the owner of the house he sends a message in these words: "The *Teacher* says, My time is at hand" (Mt 26:18; see Mk 14:14; Lk 22:11). Nicodemus had recognized that the teaching authority of Jesus was not merely human: "We know that you are a *teacher* come from God; for no one can do these signs that you do, unless God is with him" (Jn 3:2). Jesus knows that he is a different sort of Master, a unique Teacher: The scribes and Pharisees "love . . . being called rabbi by men. But you are not to be called rabbi, for you have one *teacher*, and you are all brethren. . . . Neither be called masters, for you have one *master*, the Christ" (Mt 23:6–8, 10). Those who heard the preaching of Jesus noticed the difference in his teaching: "And when Jesus finished these sayings, the crowds were astonished at his teaching, for he *taught* them as one who had authority, and not as their scribes" (Mt 7:28–29; Mk 1:22). This authority of Jesus has a very deep foundation:

> "He who rejects me and does not receive my sayings has a judge; the word that I have spoken will be his judge on the last day. For I have not spoken on my own authority; the Father who sent me has himself given me commandment what to say and what to speak. And I know that his commandment is eternal life. What I say, therefore, I say as the Father has bidden me" (Jn 12:48–50).

The words of Jesus are the words of God the Father.

Jesus has the character of Teacher or Master, and accordingly, in the New Testament, his followers are very frequently called his "disciples". There is one passage that is especially significant in this regard: "All authority in heaven and on earth has been given to me [says the risen Jesus to the eleven apostles]. Go therefore and *make disciples* of all nations, baptizing them in the name of the Father and of the Son and of the Holy Spirit, teaching them to observe all that I have commanded you; and lo, I am with you always, to the close of the age" (Mt 28:18–20). This passage shows two things. First, that the attitude of the Christian with respect to Christ is that of a disciple, of someone who is learning, of one who adheres to his teaching. Second, that the risen Jesus conferred upon his apostles the mission to teach and preach his name.

To be a disciple of Jesus Christ implies more than admitting his historical existence and accepting or acknowledging the loftiness of his moral doctrine, considering it as the teaching of an important philosopher or even of the greatest philosopher of all time. To be a disciple means to *believe* in Jesus: "Many were believing in Jesus" (see Jn 12:11). Jesus himself says: "This is the work of God, that you believe in him whom he has sent" (Jn 6:29). To believe in Jesus means acknowledging that he is the Son of God who has come into this world, following him lovingly, and accepting his word as the ultimate criterion of the Truth.

During his life, Jesus had announced that he would pass on to his disciples the work of teaching in his name: "He who hears you hears me" (Lk 10:16). As he was about to send the Twelve on a missionary journey, he said to them: "Preach as you go, saying, 'The kingdom of heaven is at hand.' . . . And if any one will not receive you or listen to your words, shake off the dust from your feet as you leave that house or town. Truly, I say to you, it shall be more tolerable on the day of judgment for the land of Sodom and Gomorrah than for that town" (Mt 10:7, 14–15). It is clear that the disciples sent by

Jesus to preach can proclaim only the gospel that he proclaimed and not their own opinions or imaginings. In this sense there are teachers in the Church: the Pope and the bishops, successors to the apostles in their mission, which they received from Jesus. The Pope and the bishops, in turn, send priests, deacons, and catechists, commissioning them to teach the faith. In a certain way, every Christian ought to give witness to the faith in words and deeds, while conforming to the gospel of the Lord and to the teaching of the Church, which is faithfully transmitted by her pastors. There is, then, a big difference between the way that Jesus is Teacher and the way in which those whom he sends teach. He is Master as the eternal Son of the Father, as eternal Wisdom; those who teach in the Church are teachers who are dependent on Jesus Christ: by the grace of the Holy Spirit they teach what he taught.

There are several other names of Christ that are related to that of MASTER or TEACHER: PROPHET, LIGHT, WITNESS, WORD OF GOD, TRUTH, and WISDOM OF GOD.

MEDIATOR

For there is one God, and there is one mediator between
God and men, the man Christ Jesus.

— I TIMOTHY 2:5

Although the word *mediator* does not appear in the Old
Testament, it is clear that in the Old Covenant there were
men who played the part of mediator or intermediary between God and the people of Israel. Moses stands out among
them (see Exodus, Numbers, and Deuteronomy). In the first
books of the Bible we very frequently read expressions such
as this: "Then the LORD said to Moses, 'Tell the people of
Israel . . .'" (Ex 14:1–2). The people, overawed by God's
terrible majesty, which was manifested on Mount Sinai, said
to Moses: "You speak to us, and we will hear; but let not
God speak to us, lest we die" (Ex 20:19). Moses was ordered
by God to hand down the law to the people (Ex 20:1–17) and
to seal God's covenant with Israel by means of sacrifice and
offering the blood of animals (Ex 24:1–8). It was Moses, too,
who organized the worship or liturgy of the Old Covenant
(Ex 25–28), and it was he who consecrated the first priests of
the Jewish people (Ex 29). The mediation of Moses consisted
in the fact that he was the lawgiver of Israel, the one who
organized the worship and established the ancient priesthood.

The Jewish priests, too, were mediators between God and
the Israelites (Lev 1—4), but this duty of mediation was
carried out in a very special way by the high priest in the
annual feast of atonement (see Lev 16:1–34). This mediation

was not limited to the ritual worship; to the priests was entrusted the preservation and teaching of the Law of God: "For the lips of a priest should guard knowledge, and men should seek instruction from his mouth, for he is the messenger of the LORD of hosts" (Mal 2:7).

This duty of mediation was entrusted by God to the prophets, as well, who were ordered to speak to the people in God's name and to announce things that would come to pass (Deut 18:9–22).

Yet these mediators were human beings, and they demonstrated at times their frailty: Moses doubted (Num 20:1–13); some priests were not very spiritual, and some were wicked (1 Sam 2:12–17; Mal 2:1–9); and cases of false prophets were not rare (Jer 14:14; 29:9).

In the New Testament, Moses is acknowledged as a mediator, albeit a transitory one: "Why then the law? It was added because of transgressions, till the offspring should come to whom the promise had been made; and it was ordained by angels through an *intermediary*" (Gal 3:19). In place of Moses, Jesus Christ comes into the world. "The covenant [that] he *mediates* is better" (Heb 8:6), and he is "the *mediator* of a new covenant, so that those who are called may receive the promised eternal inheritance, since a death has occurred which redeems them from the transgressions under the first covenant" (Heb 9:15). The first covenant was no more than the prefiguration or announcement of what was to come: "But you have come to Mount Zion and to the city of the living God, the heavenly Jerusalem, and to innumerable angels in festal gathering, and to the assembly of the first-born who are enrolled in heaven, and to a Judge who is God of all, and to the spirits of just men made perfect, and to Jesus, the *mediator* of a new covenant, and to the sprinkled blood that speaks more graciously than the blood of Abel" (Heb 12:22–24).

Jesus presents himself as the Mediator who establishes a *new* law: "Think not that I have come to abolish the law and the prophets; I have come not to abolish them but to fulfil them" (Mt 5:17). "You have heard that it was said . . . but I say to you . . ." (Mt 5:21, 27, 33, 38, 43). "This is my commandment, that you love one another as I have loved you" (Jn 15:12). Jesus, as Mediator of the New Covenant, establishes a new form of worship, which is the Eucharist, and establishes the apostles as priests of the Christian religion (see Mt 26:26–29; Mk 14:22–25; Lk 22:19–20; 1 Cor 11:23–26).

The mediating role of Jesus is unique: he is the one and only MEDIATOR because he is at the same time the Son of God, one with the Father, and a man like us, born of the Virgin Mary. If there are in the Church other sorts of mediation, such as that of the Virgin, that of the saints, and that of the priests, all of them derive their force and efficacy from the mediation of Christ. The other mediators do not add anything to the work of Jesus Christ, but, rather, they serve his mediation and are subordinate to it. In particular, the Christian priesthood does no more than make present the unique mediation of Christ.

Several names of Christ are intimately related to that of MEDIATOR: HIGH PRIEST or PONTIFF, PROPHET, SAVIOR, REDEEMER, MASTER, MESSENGER OF THE COVENANT, APOSTLE, and SHEPHERD.

PRINCE OF PEACE

For to us a child is born, to us a son is given . . . and his name
will be called ". . . Prince of Peace."

— ISAIAH 9:6

All men aspire to have peace, to live in peace. To be without
peace is a misfortune, just as to possess it is something very
close to joy and happiness. Peace is contrary not only to war,
but also to dissension. There are attitudes within man that
trouble the peace of his spirit, even if nothing is threatening
him from outside. Conversely, peaceful actions can hardly be
expected from a turbulent and agitated spirit.

The theme of peace appears frequently in the Old Testament, although the emphasis is on political and military
security with respect to Israel's neighbors, which are at times
her sworn enemies. The magnificent promise that God makes
to his people (Lev 26:3–13) contains an explicit reference to
peace: "[Y]ou shall . . . dwell in your land securely. And I
will give *peace* in the land, and you shall lie down, and none
shall make you afraid" (Lev 26:5–6); this promise is subject to
one condition: "If you walk in my statutes and observe my
commandments and do them . . ." (Lev 26:3). The solemn
words of blessing, which God himself taught the priests of
Israel, contained a promise of peace as well: "Thus you shall
bless the people of Israel: you shall say to them, The LORD
bless you and keep you: The LORD make his face to shine
upon you, and be gracious to you: The LORD lift up his
countenance upon you, and give you *peace*. So shall they [the

priests] put my name upon the people of Israel, and I will bless them" (Num 6:23–27). To wish peace was, and is to this day, the way to greet someone or say goodbye in Israel (see Gen 43:23, Douay-Rheims; Ex 4:18; Judg 6:23; 18:6; 19:20; 1 Sam 1:17; 20:42; 25:6; 29:7; 2 Sam 15:9; 2 Kings 5:19; Ezra 5:7; Jud 8:35; Tob 12:17, Douay-Rheims).

In the Psalms there are many references to peace: "May the Lord bless his people with *peace*" (Ps 29:11); "Depart from evil, and do good; seek *peace*, and pursue it" (Ps 34:14); in describing the messianic king, it is foretold: "In his days [will] righteousness flourish, and *peace* abound, till the moon be no more!" (Ps 72:7); "Great *peace* have those who love thy law; nothing can make them stumble" (Ps 119:165); it is said to Jerusalem: "He [God] makes *peace* in your borders" (Ps 147:14). The promise of peace is also a theme of the prophets, whether as a prayer of the people: "O LORD, thou wilt ordain *peace* for us" (Is 26:12); or as a prediction: "And the effect of righteousness will be *peace*, and the result of righteousness, quietness and trust for ever" (Is 32:17); or a threat: "There is no *peace*, says my God, for the wicked" (Is 57:21). The prophets stigmatized the misleading predictions of peace made by the false prophets (Jer 6:14; 8:11, 15; Ezek 13:10). Messianic times are described by Isaiah as times of peace and concord in a series of paradoxical allegories: "The wolf shall dwell with the lamb, and the leopard shall lie down with the kid, and the calf and the lion and the fatling together, and a little child shall lead them. The cow and the bear shall feed; their young shall lie down together; and the lion shall eat straw like the ox" (Is 11:6–7). These messianic times will come to pass with the coming of the Messiah, of whom it is said: "For to us a child is born, to us a son is given; and the government will be upon his shoulder, and his name will be called 'Wonderful Counselor, Mighty God, Everlasting Father, *Prince of Peace.*' Of the increase of his

government and of *peace* there will be no end, upon the
throne of David, and over his kingdom, to establish it, and to
uphold it with justice and with righteousness from this time
forth and for evermore. The zeal of the LORD of hosts will do
this" (Is 9:6–7).

Zechariah the priest, father of the Baptist, announced
Christ, saying: "[T]he day shall dawn upon us from on high
to give light to those who sit in darkness and in the shadow of
death, to guide our feet into the way of *peace*" (Lk 1:78–79).
Saint Paul describes the salvific activity of Christ as a work of
peace:

> But now in Christ Jesus you who once were far off have been
> brought near in the blood of Christ. For he is our *peace*, who
> has made us both [= the Jews and the Gentiles] one, and has
> broken down the dividing wall of hostility, by abolishing in
> his flesh the [Mosaic] law of commandments and ordinances,
> that he might create in himself one new man in place of the
> two [peoples], so making *peace*, and might reconcile us both
> to God in one body through the cross, thereby bringing the
> hostility to an end. And he came and preached *peace* to you
> who were far off and *peace* to those who were near; for
> through him we both have access in one Spirit to the Father"
> (Eph 2:13–18).

In this passage, there are two levels of peace: one refers to
the end of the difference between Jews and non-Jews, a
difference that in the future will be irrelevant for salvation
(Gal 3:28; Col 3:11); and another refers to reconciliation with
God by means of the Cross of Christ: "Since we are justified
by faith, we have *peace* with God through our Lord Jesus
Christ" (Rom 5:1), who reconciles all things, "*making peace
through the blood of his cross*" (Col 1:20).

Jesus himself explicitly proposes the theme of peace. Thus,
in the beatitudes, he declares: "Blessed are the *peacemakers*;
for they shall be called sons of God" (Mt 5:9). If a Christian

can and ought to be a peacemaker, this is because he has heard Christ, who says: "*Peace* I leave with you; my *peace* I give to you; not as the world gives do I give to you. Let not your hearts be troubled, neither let them be afraid" (Jn 14:27). The peace that Jesus has in his heart originates in the fact that the Father is with him, and so our peace is based on the fact that Christ is with us: "I am not alone, for the Father is with me. I have said this to you, that in me you may have *peace*. In the world you have tribulation; but be of good cheer, I have overcome the world" (Jn 16:32–33); and "I am with you always, to the close of the age" (Mt 28:20). The peace the world offers is often based on compromises, evasion, deals, and ambiguities, when it is not dependent upon the capability of each party to terrify the other and thus to deter it from the use of force. The world's peace is external, and many times it does not proceed from a peace-ful and peaceable heart. That is not the peace of Christ, which is, above all, interior and spiritual. This peace is far removed from ambiguity: "Let what you say be simply 'Yes' or 'No'" (Mt 5:37); in no way does it exclude the possibility and obligation of taking a courageous and decisive stand, as Christ did when he unmasked the scribes and the Pharisees (Mt 23:1–33; Mk 12:38–40; Lk 20:45–47); or when he cleansed the Temple in Jerusalem of the money-changers (Mt 21:12–13; Mk 11:15–17; Lk 19:45). Christian peace does not mean disguising the truth or becoming ac-complices to wrongdoing through a guilty silence. This is what the apostles Peter and John understood when members of the Jewish Sanhedrin "called them and charged them not to speak or teach at all in the name of Jesus. But Peter and John answered them, 'Whether it is right in the sight of God to listen to you rather than to God, you must judge; for we cannot but speak of what we have seen and heard'" (Acts 4:18–20). These characteristics of the peace of Christ serve also to explain other words of his, which at first appear to be disconcerting:

> "Do not think that I have come to bring peace on earth; I have not come to bring peace, but a sword. For I have come to set a man against his father, and a daughter against her mother, and a daughter-in-law against her mother-in-law; and a man's foes will be those of his own household. He who loves father or mother more than me is not worthy of me; and he who loves son or daughter more than me is not worthy of me" (Mt 10:34–37; see Lk 12:51–53).

The division that Jesus speaks of will be that which is caused by the rejection of his teaching: "Remember the word that I said to you, 'A servant is not greater than his master.' If they persecuted me, they will persecute you" (Jn 15:20). "Then they will deliver you up to tribulation, and put you to death; and you will be hated by all nations for my name's sake" (Mt 24:9).

There are various instruments or methods of peace. First of all, constantly putting into practice the saying of Christ: "As you wish that men would do to you, do so to them" (Lk 6:31; see an alternative formulation in Mt 7:12 and its biblical origin in Tob 4:15). Then, fulfilling the precept of the Lord: "Love your enemies and pray for those who persecute you, so that you may be sons of your Father who is in heaven; for he makes his sun rise on the evil and on the good, and sends rain on the just and on the unjust" (Mt 5:44–45; Lk 6:27–30), which implies a willingness to forgive, without which we cannot expect God to forgive us either (Mt 6:12, 14–15). It is also an instrument of peace to acknowledge one's own errors: "[F]irst take the log out of your own eye, and then you will see clearly to take the speck out of your brother's eye" (Mt 7:5); and to have love for the truth that makes us really free (Jn 8:32), since peace is often disturbed by lying or by the stubbornness that refuses to

accept that the other person might be at least partly right.
Finally, the work of peace is carried out by those who are
merciful and meek (Mt 5:5, 7). It is not at all surprising that
Saint Paul sees in a peaceful spirit one of the requisite gifts
for the ministers who have responsibility in the Church: "A
bishop must be . . . not violent but gentle, not quarrelsome"
(1 Tim 3:2–3); "he must not be quick-tempered or violent"
(Tit 1:7).

We can gather how important peace is for the Church and
for mankind from the fact that Christ greeted his followers by
wishing them peace (Mk 5:34; Lk 7:50; 8:48; Jn 20:21, 26)
and taught them to greet one another with a blessing of peace
(Mt 10:12; Lk 10:5). This example and this command explain
the apostolic custom of the salutation of peace: "To all God's
beloved in Rome, who are called to be saints: Grace to you
and *peace* from God our Father and the Lord Jesus Christ"
(Rom 1:7; see also 1 Cor 1:3; 2 Cor 1:2; Gal 1:3; Eph 1:2;
6:23; Phil 1:2; Col 1:2; 1 Thess 1:1; 2 Thess 3:16; 1 Tim 1:2;
2 Tim 1:2; Tit 1:4; Philem 3; 1 Pet 1:2; 2 Pet 1:2; 2 Jn 3; 3 Jn
15; Rev 1:4).

The name PRINCE OF PEACE is in keeping with the song of
the angels at the birth of Jesus: "Glory to God in the highest,
and on earth *peace* among men with whom he is pleased" (Lk
2:14); and the name corresponds to the will of Christ for his
own: "Have salt in yourselves, and be at *peace* with one
another" (Mk 9:50). Related to this title are the names of
MEDIATOR, SHEPHERD, KING, TRUTH, HIGH PRIEST, JESUS,
and REDEEMER.

PROPHET

"This is the prophet Jesus from Nazareth of Galilee."

— MATTHEW 21:11

No one who has browsed even a little in Sacred Scripture can fail to notice the enormous importance that the prophets had in the Old Testament. They appear also, though with less frequency, in the New Testament.

In eulogizing Moses, the Bible says:

> And there has not arisen a *prophet* since in Israel like Moses, whom the LORD knew face to face, none like him for all the signs and the wonders which the LORD sent him to do in the land of Egypt, to Pharaoh and to all his servants and to all his land, and for all the mighty power and all the great and terrible deeds which Moses wrought in the sight of all Israel (Deut 34:10–12).

> [T]he Lord brought forth a man of mercy... beloved by God and man, Moses, whose memory is blessed. He made him equal in glory to the holy ones, and made him great in the fears of his enemies. By his words he caused signs to cease; the Lord glorified him in the presence of kings. He gave him commands for his people, and showed him part of his glory. He sanctified him through faithfulness and meekness; he chose him out of all mankind. He made him hear his voice, and led him into the thick darkness, and gave him the commandments face to face, the law of life and knowledge, to teach Jacob the covenant, and Israel his judgments (Sir 45:1–5).

Joshua, the leader of the people after the death of Moses, is distinguished for being "the successor of Moses in *prophesying*" (Sir 46:1). In the history of Israel there are many eminent prophets: Samuel (1 and 2 Sam), Elijah and Elisha (1 and 2 Kings), Isaiah, Jeremiah, Ezekiel, Daniel, Hosea, Malachi, and many others, including some whose names have not come down to us. The presence and activity of the prophets in Israel guaranteed not only a knowledge of God's plans with regard to the prediction of future events, but also, and principally, an understanding of his judgments with regard to the fidelity or infidelity of the people. The absence of prophets is one of the signs of the desolation of Israel: "[T]here is no longer any *prophet*" (Ps 74:9). It is interesting to note that, especially in the book of Jeremiah, the prophets and the priests are usually named together (see, for example, Jer 6:13; 8:10; 14:18; 26:7). Yet Israel came to know the plague of false prophets, too: "An appalling and horrible thing has happened in the land: *the prophets prophesy falsely*, and the priests rule at their direction; my people love to have it so" (Jer 5:30–31). "Do not listen to the words of the *prophets* who prophesy to you, filling you with vain hopes; they speak visions of their own minds, not from the mouth of the LORD. . . . I did not send the *prophets*, yet they ran; I did not speak to them, yet they prophesied" (Jer 23:16, 21; see the entire chapter). This is why God says: "Behold, I am against those who *prophesy lying dreams*, and who tell them and lead my people astray by their lies and their recklessness, when I did not send them or charge them; so they do not profit this people at all, says the LORD" (Jer 23:32).

When John the Baptist was born, his father, the priest Zechariah, prophesied (Lk 1:67). When Joseph and Mary presented the child Jesus in the temple, prophesy was present as well: the old man Simeon prophesied (although the Gospel does not use this word, Lk 1:25–35), and so did the aged

Anna, of whom the Gospel says explicitly that she was a prophetess (Lk 2:36–39). John the Baptist would be called *"the prophet of the Most High*; for you will go before the Lord to prepare his ways, to give knowledge of salvation to his people in the forgiveness of their sins" (Lk 1:76–77), according to the prophecy of his father. Jesus says of his cousin John the Baptist that he is *a prophet* and *more than a prophet* (Mt 11:9), and the Jewish people held him as such (Mt 21:26). When the Jews asked John whether he was *the* Prophet, he replied that he was not (Jn 1:21, 24), perhaps out of humility, or maybe because he wanted to avoid any possible misunderstanding, since the name of Prophet was a messianic title, and there were some who thought he might be the Messiah (Lk 3:15). The preaching of John the Baptist was entirely in the style of the ancient prophets (see Mt 3:7–10; Mk 1:7–8; Lk 3:1–14). Even his censure of Herod, on account of the king's incestuous adultery, was a prophetic act (see Mt 14:1–5; Mk 6:17–20; Lk 3:19). "So, with many other exhortations, he [John] preached good news to the people" (Lk 3:18). These words accentuate the similarity between the prophesying and evangelization, which is one reason why the ministry of the word in the Church is commonly referred to as her "prophetic mission". The authenticity of the Baptist's prophetic ministry is seen in his complete lack of interest in his own glory and in his total consecration to proclaiming Christ: "He [Christ] must increase; but I must decrease" (Jn 3:30). John died at Herod's command because of his fidelity to his prophetic ministry: he was a faithful witness (Jn 1:34) and a martyr because of his testimony.

Moses had said: "The LORD your God will raise up for you a *prophet* like me from among you [from among the people of Israel], from your brethren—him you shall heed . . . ," for "the LORD said to me, '. . . I will raise up for them a *prophet* like you from among their brethren; and I will put my words in his mouth, and he shall speak to them all that I command him" (Deut 18:15, 17–18). These words were fulfilled in the prophets of Israel, but their full meaning would become a reality only in Jesus Christ (Acts 3:22; 7:37). The Jewish people, unlike the Pharisees and the Herodians, "held him [Jesus] to be a *prophet*" (Mt 21:46). "But others said [about Jesus], 'It is Elijah.' And others said, 'It is a *prophet*, like one of the *prophets* of old'" (Mk 6:15). When Jesus raised from the dead the son of the widow of Nain, the people "glorified God, saying, 'A great *prophet* has arisen among us!' and 'God has visited his people!'" (Lk 7:16); but the Pharisees refused to recognize Jesus as a prophet: "If this man were a *prophet* . . ." (Lk 7:39). The Samaritan woman, also, whom Jesus met at Jacob's well, said to him: "Sir, I perceive that you are a *prophet*" (Jn 4:19); and the man who had been blind from birth and was cured by Jesus gave the same testimony. When the Pharisees asked him: "What do you say about him, since he has opened your eyes?", he replied, "He is a *prophet*" (Jn 9:17). There are testimonies that are even more explicit. After the multiplication of the loaves, "when the people saw the sign which he [Jesus] had done, they said, 'This is indeed the *prophet* who is to come into the world!'" (Jn 6:14); and on another occasion, after listening to him, some of the people said, "This is really the *prophet*" (Jn 7:40). Jesus himself declared, albeit indirectly, that he was a prophet. In Nazareth, faced with the disbelief of his compatriots, he told them: "A *prophet* is not without honor except in his own country and in his own house" (Mt 13:57; Mk 6:4; Lk 4:24–27; Jn 4:44). The extraordinary and unique character of Christ's prophetic ministry is clear from his own words: "He who comes from heaven is above all. He bears witness to what he has seen and heard, yet no one receives his testimony; he who receives his testimony sets his seal to this, that God is true. For he whom God has sent utters the words of God, for it is not by measure that he gives the Spirit" (Jn 3:31–34).

No one can be a prophet as Jesus is Prophet, because he alone is the Son and the Word of the Father. If it was said of Moses that he spoke with God face to face, then that is even more true of the Word of God, who from the beginning "was with God, and . . . was God" (Jn 1:1). Jesus warned his disciples against false prophets, pointing out that they can be distinguished from the true prophets by their fruits (Mt 7:15–20). Ancient testimony from shortly after the Resurrection tells us that the first disciples gave Jesus the title of prophet: the two disciples on the way to Emmaus say to Jesus, who joins them as they are walking, without their recognizing him immediately: " 'Are you the only visitor to Jerusalem who does not know the things that have happened there in these days?' And he said to them, 'What things?' And they said to him, 'Concerning Jesus of Nazareth, who was a *prophet* mighty in deed and word before God and all the people . . .' " (Lk 24:18–19).

When the Holy Spirit descended upon the disciples on the day of Pentecost, bestowing upon them the gift of tongues, Saint Peter proclaimed in the presence of the Jews:

> This is what was spoken by the prophet Joel: "And in the last days it shall be, God declares, that I will pour out my Spirit upon all flesh, and your sons and your daughters *shall prophesy*, and your young men shall see visions, and your old men shall dream dreams; yea, and on my menservants and my maidservants in those days I will pour out my Spirit; and they *shall prophesy*" (Acts 2:16–18; Joel 2:28–29).

The Book of Acts says that "in the Church at Antioch there were *prophets* and teachers" (Acts 13:1); to them God revealed the mission entrusted to Barnabas and Saul, who, in the city of Paphos, on the island of Cyprus, encountered a Jewish false prophet (Acts 13:6,) whom they unmasked. In Ephesus, Saint Paul baptized some disciples who had received John's baptism only, and, when he laid hands upon them, "the Holy Spirit came on them; and they spoke with tongues and *prophesied*" (Acts 19:1–7). We read also in the Acts of the Apostles that, during one of Saint Paul's journeys to Jerusalem: "[We] came to Caesarea; and we entered the house of Philip the evangelist, who was one of the seven [selected to assist the Apostles, Acts 6:1ff.], and stayed with him. And he had four unmarried daughters, who *prophesied*. While we were staying for some days, a *prophet* named Agabus came down from Judea" (Acts 21:8–11), who foretold Paul's next imprisonment. This prophet, Agabus, belonged to a group of prophets based in Jerusalem (Acts 11:27–28). The names Judas and Silas have also come down to us; they were prophets in Antioch (Acts 15:32). It would appear that the presence and activity of prophets were commonplace in the early Church communities, and that is why Saint Paul mentions prophets as one of the categories of ministers in the Christian communities (1 Cor 12:28; Eph 2:20; 4:11) and establishes norms for the exercise of their office (1 Cor 11:4; 12:29; 14:1–40). By the second century, the name of "prophet" is no longer listed among the formal activities of the Church, but that does not mean that the Church's prophetic ministry disappeared; rather, it is incorporated in the magisterial or teaching mission of the legitimate pastors of the Church. Yet there have also been men and women who, filled with and moved by the Spirit of Christ in a special way, have been authentic bearers of the prophetic charism, whether or not they were pastors of the Church. We could mention the names of Saint Ignatius of Antioch, Saint Francis of Assisi, Saint Catherine of Siena, Saint Vincent Ferrer, Saint Francis Xavier, Saint Teresa of Avila, and Saint John Bosco, among many others.

Consecrated life—the profession of the evangelical counsels of poverty, obedience, and chastity—can also be considered a prophetic testimony within the Church. There have been acts of the Church's Magisterium that have had a prophetic character, for example, the encyclical *Rerum Novarum* of Pope Leo XIII and the encyclical *Humanae Vitae* of Paul VI, to which Pope John Paul II has expressly attributed prophetic significance.

On concluding these reflections on the name PROPHET, it is appropriate to say something about the difference between the prophetic charism in the Old Testament, that is, in the people of Israel, and the charism in the Christian Church. In Israel, authentic prophecy was a kind of supreme doctrinal authority: the prophet urged people to follow the law, issued commandments in the name of God, and, in many cases, had the charism of divine inspiration, that is, he was used by God as an instrument to write the sacred books of the Bible. Even the Jewish priests and the high priests were reprimanded by the prophets. In Israel, there was no authentic magisterium entrusted exclusively to priests. It is different in the Church: Christ entrusted to Peter and to the other apostles and to their successors, the Pope and the bishops, a Magisterium that is not only authentic, but also in many cases infallible, a teaching office that is charged with preserving and proclaiming the genuine meaning of Christian revelation and the gospel message. To this Magisterium belongs the discernment of the charisms that the Holy Spirit stirs up in the Church, among them the prophetic charism. When a man rises up, allegedly in the name of Christ, against the Magisterium of the Church, claiming to have a prophetic charism, he is a false prophet. Yet pastors must take care to consider the prophetic gift that sometimes appears in the Church, because through it the movement of the Holy Spirit becomes perceptible—the Spirit who speaks to the

Church not only through her hierarchy, but also through humble and holy persons whose testimony usually appears disconcerting, especially at first.

The name of PROPHET is related to the names of TEACHER, WITNESS, TRUTH, LIGHT, MEDIATOR, and WORD.

REDEEMER

"The Son of man came . . . to serve, and to give his life
as a ransom for many."

— MARK 10:45

The idea of "salvation" has an interesting biblical nuance that
is expressed by the word REDEMPTION. In the Old Testament,
the word *redemption* very often applies to the situation in
which something that, for some reason, has passed from
someone's domain or property returns to his control through
the payment of a ransom, which is made to the individual to
whom the person or the object has been subjected or handed
over. In Israel, the following were liable to "redemption":
firstborn males (see Ex 13:1–16), lands (Lev 25:23–34), persons who have been enslaved (Lev 25:39–55), persons who
have made a vow consecrating themselves to Yahweh (Lev
27:1–8), animals and objects consecrated to God (Lev 27:9–
33). But Israel herself was "redeemed" by Yahweh: "It is
because the LORD loves you, and is keeping the oath which he
swore to your fathers, that the LORD has brought you out
with a mighty hand, and *redeemed you* from the house of
bondage, from the hand of Pharaoh king of Egypt" (Deut
7:8). The implication is that Israel, which belonged to Yahweh, had been subjugated by the Egyptians; from this slavery
God frees her, in this case without paying anything to the
oppressors. This salvation or liberation constitutes a new title,
in virtue of which the Israelite people are the property or
inheritance of the Lord. The prophets, too, employ the word

redemption to refer to Israel's political liberation from the nations that oppressed her after the glorious reigns of David and Solomon (see, for example, Is 1:27; 43:1; 48:20; Jer 15:21; 31:11). One sign of the messianic times will be the accomplishment of a redemption without payment of a ransom, as Israel had been redeemed from the power of the Egyptians (Is 52:1–6). Already in the Old Testament there is talk of "redemption" with respect to sin: "Wherefore, O King [says Daniel to Nebuchadnezzar], let my counsel be acceptable to thee, and *redeem* thou thy sins with alms [justice], and thy iniquities with works of mercy to the poor: perhaps he will forgive thy offences" (Dan 4:24, Douay-Rheims). This passage implies that sin subjects man to a kind of slavery, from which he can be freed by paying a ransom in the form of almsgiving to the poor. In any case, God is always the great redeemer or "rescuer": "Let the words of my mouth and the meditation of my heart be acceptable in thy sight, O LORD, my rock and my *redeemer*" (Ps 19:14); "I will help you [Israel], says the LORD; your *Redeemer* is the Holy One of Israel" (Is 41:14. Note that in John 6:69 Peter says to Jesus, "[W]e have believed, and have come to know, that you are the Holy One of God"). As a reminder, perhaps, of his saving power, God is sometimes called "the Redeemer, the Mighty One" (Is 49:26; 60:16; see Jer 50:34).

At the dawn of the New Testament, the Jewish priest Zechariah, father of John the Baptist, "was filled with the Holy Spirit, and prophesied, saying, 'Blessed be the Lord God of Israel, for he has visited and *redeemed* his people'" (Lk 1:67–68). In Zechariah's canticle, this mention of redemption is followed by other references, in the same context, to salvation (vv. 69, 71) and to deliverance (v. 74), with special emphasis upon holiness: "[T]hat we . . . might serve him without fear, in holiness and righteousness before him all the days of our life", since the Baptist is coming "to give knowledge of salvation to his people in the forgiveness of their sins . . ." (vv. 74–75, 77).

Although, in the New Testament, the name of Redeemer is not given to Jesus directly, our redemption is explicitly attributed to him. He himself declares that he had come "to give his life as a *ransom* for many" (Mt 20:28; Mk 10:45), a testimony frequently taken up by Saint Paul: Christ "gave himself as a *ransom* for all" (1 Tim 2:6); "all have sinned and fall short of the glory of God, [and now] they are justified by his grace as a gift, through the *redemption* which is in Christ Jesus, whom God put forward as an expiation by his blood, to be received by faith" (Rom 3:23–25); "Christ *redeemed* us from the curse of the law, having become a curse for us—for it is written, 'Cursed be every one who hangs on a tree'" (Gal 3:13);

> For the grace of God has appeared for the salvation of all men, training us to renounce irreligion and worldly passions, and to live sober, upright, and godly lives in this world, awaiting our blessed hope, the appearing of the glory of our great God and Savior Jesus Christ, who gave himself for us to *redeem us* [= ransom us] from all iniquity and to purify for himself a people of his own who are zealous for good deeds (Tit 2:11–14).

In Christ "we have *redemption*" (Eph 1:7; Col 1:14). The Letter to the Hebrews assures us that this redemption, or ransom, accomplished by Christ is eternal (Heb 9:12ff.). The elders of the Book of Revelation "sang a new song, saying, 'Worthy art thou to take the scroll and to open its seals, for thou [Christ, the Lamb] wast slain and by thy blood didst *ransom* men for God from every tribe and tongue and people and nation . . .'" (Rev 5:9). Saint Peter also uses this expression:

> And if you invoke as Father him who judges each one impartially according to his deeds, conduct yourselves with

fear throughout the time of your exile. You know that you were *ransomed* from the futile ways inherited from your fathers, not with perishable things such as silver or gold, but with the precious blood of Christ, like that of a lamb without blemish or spot . . . so that your faith and hope are in God (1 Pet 1:17–21).

It is clear that the blood of Christ, the "price" of our redemption, is not "paid" to the devil, who had dominion over mankind because of sin; the devil is not the legitimate owner of men but a usurper, just as the Egyptians were not the masters of Israel but their unjust oppressors. The blood of Christ, offered to the Father as a sacrifice of praise and as a supreme proof of love through his obedience unto death, even death on a Cross, redeems us by making amends for our acts of disobedience and by meriting for us the grace of filial adoption, which results in deliverance from the power of Satan, to whom sin subjects and enslaves us.

The name of REDEEMER has affinities with the names of SAVIOR, LAMB, SERVANT, and MEDIATOR.

ROCK

The Rock was Christ.

— I CORINTHIANS 10:4

The word ROCK, as a proper name of Christ, has precedents in the Old Testament: "For he will hide me in his shelter in the day of trouble; he will conceal me under the cover of his tent, he will set me high upon a *rock*" (Ps 27:5). "Therefore thus says the Lord GOD, 'Behold, I am laying in Zion for a foundation a *stone*, a tested *stone*, a precious *cornerstone*, of a sure foundation: He who believes will not be in haste'" (Is 28:16).

> Hear now, O Joshua the high priest, you and your friends who sit before you, for they are men of good omen: behold, I will bring my servant the Branch. For behold, upon the *stone* which I have set before Joshua, upon a *single stone* with seven facets, I will engrave its inscription, says the LORD of hosts, and I will remove the guilt of this land in a single day (Zech 3:8–9).

> "You saw, O king, and behold, a great image [statue]. This image, mighty and of exceeding brightness, stood before you, and its appearance was frightening. The head of this image was of fine gold, its breast and arms of silver, its belly and thighs of bronze, its legs of iron, its feet partly of iron and partly of clay. As you looked, a *stone* was cut out by no human hand, and it smote the image on its feet of iron and clay, and broke them in pieces; then the iron, the clay, the bronze, the silver, and the gold, all together were broken in pieces, and

became like the chaff of the summer threshing floors; and the wind carried them away, so that not a trace of them could be found. But the *stone* that struck the image became a great mountain and filled the whole earth. . . . And in the days of those kings the God of heaven will set up a kingdom which shall never be destroyed, nor shall its sovereignty be left to another people. It shall break in pieces all these kingdoms and bring them to an end, and it shall stand for ever; just as you saw that a *stone* was cut from a mountain by no human hand, and that it broke in pieces the iron, the bronze, the clay, the silver, and the gold" (Dan 2:31–45).

The tradition of the Church has seen these stones as figures of Christ. He is the refuge, he is the sole foundation, he is the cornerstone, through him iniquity vanishes, he fills the whole earth. "Let each man take care how he builds. . . . For no other *foundation* can any one lay than that which is laid, which is Jesus Christ" (1 Cor 3:10–11).

Jesus called himself ROCK, saying:

"Have you never read in the scriptures: 'The very *stone* which the builders rejected has become the head of the corner [cornerstone]; this was the Lord's doing, and it is marvelous in our eyes'? Therefore I tell you, the kingdom of God will be taken away from you and given to a nation producing the fruits of it. And he who falls on this stone will be broken to pieces; but when it falls on any one, it will crush him" (Mt 21:42–44; see Mk 12:10; Lk 20:17–18).

The passage cited by Jesus here is Psalm 118:22–23, and he applies it to the rejection that he received at the hands of the Jews; this same passage is quoted by Saint Peter before the Sanhedrin: "This is the *stone* which rejected by you builders, but which has become the head of the corner [*cornerstone*]. And there is salvation in no one else, for there is no other name under heaven given among men by which we must be saved" (Acts 4:11–12).

In the earliest apostolic preaching, Christ is referred to several times by the name of Stone. Saint Paul, referring to the rejection of Christ by the Jews, says that "they have stumbled over the stumbling *stone*, as it is written, 'Behold, I am laying in Zion a *stone* that will make men stumble, a *rock* that will make them fall; and he who believes in him will not be put to shame'" (Rom 9:32–33); the theme of the "stumbling stone" is similar to that of the "sign of contradiction" foretold by Simeon (Lk 2:34). Addressing the faithful, Saint Paul tells them that they are:

> . . . fellow citizens with the saints and members of the household of God, built upon the *foundation* of the apostles and prophets, Christ Jesus himself being the *cornerstone*, in whom the whole structure is joined together and grows into a holy temple in the Lord; in whom you also are built into it for a dwelling place of God in the Spirit (Eph 2:19–22).

In speaking about the Israelites in the desert, Paul says that "all ate the same supernatural food and all drank the same supernatural drink. For they drank from the supernatural *Rock* which followed them, and the *Rock* was Christ" (1 Cor 10:3–4). Saint Peter also employs this name of "Rock" or "Stone":

> Come to him [Christ], to that living *stone*, rejected by men but in God's sight chosen and precious; and like living *stones* be yourselves built into a spiritual house. . . . For it stands in scripture: "Behold, I am laying in Zion a *stone*, a *cornerstone* chosen and precious, and he who believes in him will not be put to shame." To you therefore who believe, he is precious, but for those who do not believe, "The very *stone* which the builders rejected has become the head of the corner," and "A *stone* that will make men stumble, a *rock* that will make them fall" (1 Pet 2:4–8).

As we can see, the theme of the stone or rock is quite rich: it suggests that Christ is the bedrock and the only foundation;

that salvation depends on man's position in regard to Christ; that the Church, as the temple or house of God, is built upon Christ; that Christ is the source from which all spiritual drink flows (see Jn 7:37ff.). It is interesting to note that the passage by Saint Peter indicates that the quality of Rock that belongs to Christ is, in a certain way, communicated to his disciples, who then become living stones as well in the structure of the Church.

There is one very special instance of Christ communicating to another his office of Rock:

> Now when Jesus came into the district of Caesarea Philippi, he asked his disciples, "Who do men say that the Son of man is?" And they said, "Some say John the Baptist, others say Elijah, and others Jeremiah or one of the prophets." He said to them, "But who do you say that I am?" Simon Peter replied, "You are the Christ, the Son of the living God." And Jesus answered him, "Blessed are you, Simon Bar-Jona! For flesh and blood has not revealed this to you, but my Father who is in heaven. And I tell you, you are Peter, and on this *rock* I will build my church, and the powers of death shall not prevail against it" (Mt 16:13–18).

There is no doubt that Simon received from Jesus the name of Peter: "Jesus looked at him, and said, 'So you are Simon the son of John? You shall be called *Cephas*' (which means *Peter*)" (Jn 1:42). Saint Paul uses the Aramaic word *Cephas* several times instead of its translation, "Peter", to refer to the Prince of the Apostles (1 Cor 1:12; 3:22; 9:5; 15:5; Gal 2:9, 14). This name, given to Simon by Christ, points out his role as the visible head of the Church: "I will give you the keys of the kingdom of heaven, and whatever you bind on earth shall be bound in heaven, and whatever you loose on earth shall be loosed in heaven" (Mt 16:19). In quite a number of passages in the New Testament it is evident that Peter effectively discharges the duties of the head of the disciples and of the

Church (see Jn 6:68–69; 20:3–7; 21:15–19; Lk 22:31–34; Acts 1:15–26; 5:1–11; 12:4ff; 15:1–32; 1 Cor 15:4–5). The Catholic faith recognizes Saint Peter and his successors, the bishops of Rome, as the visible Head of the Church. It acknowledges their authority to make definitions of faith and to govern the whole Church. This does not mean denying the position of Stone or Rock, which belongs in a unique sense to Christ; if someone were to deny it, he would no longer be a Christian. To acknowledge Peter and the Pope means nothing other than to believe that Jesus Christ, risen from the dead and ascended in heaven, performs to a certain extent his function as Rock of the Church by means of his vicar or representative, since in a complete and absolute sense Christ, and he alone, is the foundation stone of the Church.

The name of ROCK suggests firmness, certainty, permanence, a refuge from the wind and the waves, the groundwork of a building: all this we have in Christ. Related to this name are the names of TEACHER, HEAD, and TRUTH.

SHEPHERD or PASTOR

"I am the good shepherd."

— JOHN 10:11

The image of the shepherd was familiar to the Jewish contemporaries of Jesus: shepherding was a well-known and
widespread activity (see Lk 2:8), particularly in the arid re-
gions of Judah. The Old Testament describes many men who
were shepherds, and the position of shepherd serves as a
symbol or a model for those whose duty it is to watch over
the people, although this very often emerges from bitter
complaints about the bad shepherds who "have no understanding [and] have all turned to their own way" (Is 56:11),
who rebelled against God (see Jer 2:8), "who destroy and
scatter the sheep" (Jer 23:1), who have led the sheep astray
(see Jer 50:6), "who have been feeding [them]selves" (Ezek
34:2ff.). The plight of the people is expressed through a
comparison to sheep without a shepherd (Num 27:17; 1
Kings 22:17; 2 Chron 18:16; Jud 11:19; Zech 10:2).

In the Old Testament, God himself claims the name of
SHEPHERD of Israel: "Behold your God! . . . He will feed his
flock like a *shepherd*, he will gather the lambs in his arms, he
will carry them in his bosom, and gently lead those that are
with young" (Is 40:9, 11).

> For thus says the Lord GOD: Behold, I, I myself will search
> for my sheep, and will seek them out. As a *shepherd* seeks out
> his flock when some of his sheep have been scattered abroad,
> so will I seek out my sheep; and I will rescue them. . . . I will

bring them . . . into their own land; . . . I will feed them with
good pasture. . . . I myself will be the shepherd of my sheep.
. . . I will seek the lost, and I will bring back the strayed, and
I will bind up the crippled, and I will strengthen the weak.
. . . I will feed them in justice . . . [and will] judge between
sheep and sheep (Ezek 34:11–17).

Already in the Old Testament the name of shepherd has a
messianic meaning. Of King Cyrus, who restored Israel, God
says, "He is my *shepherd*" (Is 44:28); Cyrus was a prefigure-
ment of the true restoration in Christ. This is evident in
the words of Ezekiel: "And I will set up over them [over
my sheep] one *shepherd*, my servant David, and he shall feed
them: he shall feed them and be their *shepherd*" (Ezek 34:23).
Now, when Ezekiel was writing, King David was already long
dead, and consequently the words of the prophet could refer
only to the Messiah, David's descendant (1 Chron 17:11ff.).
In this way the messianic titles of "Shepherd" and "Son of
David" are connected.

In the description of the Last Judgment, Jesus portrays himself as the shepherd who will separate the sheep from the goats
(Mt 25:33), a theme that closely resembles the one in Ezekiel
34:16–17. When Jesus was arrested in the garden on the
Mount of Olives, he recalled that the prophesy of Zechariah
was thereby fulfilled: "Strike the shepherd, that the sheep may
be scattered" (Zech 13:7; see Mt 26:31 and Mk 14:27).

Yet the most extensive passage in which Jesus speaks of
himself as SHEPHERD is the one found in chapter 10 of the
Gospel of Saint John. After the first part of the text, in which
Jesus portrays himself as the true Door of the flock (a theme
that also belongs to pastoral life, vv. 1–9), the theme of the
Good Shepherd is developed (vv. 11–16):

"I am the Good *Shepherd*. The good *shepherd* lays down his
life for the sheep. He who is a hireling and not a *shepherd*,

whose own the sheep are not, sees the wolf coming and leaves the sheep and flees; and the wolf snatches them and scatters them. He flees because he is a hireling and cares nothing for the sheep. I [on the other hand] am the good shepherd; I know my own [sheep] and my own know me, as the Father knows me and I know the Father; and I lay down my life for the sheep. And I have other sheep, that are not of this fold; I must bring them also, and they will heed my voice. So there shall be one flock, one *shepherd*" (Jn 10:11–16).

The point of this beautiful passage is that the Good Shepherd loves his sheep so much that he is willing to risk and even give up his own life in order to defend them. The hireling, instead, is interested only in his pay, and if he cares at all for the sheep, it is not out of love or to the point of sacrificing himself for them. Without mentioning the word *shepherd*, the parable of the lost sheep (see Mt 18:12–14 and Lk 15:3–7) suggests the same idea of the shepherd's earnest and self-sacrificing care for his flock, especially for the sheep who have strayed; that is to say, it presents the image of the compassionate, merciful shepherd, as he had been described already by the prophet Ezekiel (34:16ff.).

In contrast with the love of the Good Shepherd, Scripture describes the odious characteristics of the bad shepherds:

Son of man, prophesy against the *shepherds* of Israel, prophesy, and say to them, even to the shepherds, Thus says the Lord GOD: Ho, *shepherds* of Israel who have been feeding yourselves! Should not *shepherds* feed the sheep? You eat the fat, you clothe yourselves with the wool, you slaughter the fatlings; but you do not feed the sheep. The weak you have not strengthened, the sick you have not healed, the crippled you have not bound up, the strayed you have not brought back, the lost you have not sought, and with force and harshness you have ruled them. So they were scattered, because there was no *shepherd*; and they became food for all the wild beasts. My sheep were scattered, they wandered over all the mountains and on every high hill; my sheep were scattered over all the face of the earth, with none to search or seek for them. Therefore, you *shepherds*, hear the word of the LORD: As I live, says the Lord GOD, because my sheep have become a prey, and my sheep have become food for all the wild beasts, since there was no *shepherd*; and because my *shepherds* have not searched for my sheep, but the *shepherds* have fed themselves, and have not fed my sheep; therefore, you *shepherds*, hear the word of the LORD: Thus says the Lord GOD, Behold, I am *against the shepherds*; and I will require my sheep at their hand, and put a stop to their feeding the sheep; no longer shall the *shepherds* feed themselves. I will rescue my sheep from their mouths, that they may not be food for them (Ezek 34:2–10).

The title of Shepherd, which Jesus himself had claimed, was applied to him from the earliest Christian era. The Letter to the Hebrews refers to "the great *shepherd* of the sheep, our Lord Jesus" (Heb 13:20), whereas the First Letter of Saint Peter says that Jesus "bore our sins in his body on the tree [of the Cross], that we might die to sin and live to righteousness. By his wounds you have been healed. For you were straying like sheep, but have now returned to the *Shepherd* and Guardian of your souls" (1 Pet 2:24–25).

That Jesus himself entrusted to Peter the task of feeding his sheep (Jn 21:14–17) explains why the title of "pastor" was very soon applied to the ministers of the Church. The same Letter of Saint Peter just cited addresses the elders, saying to them: "*Tend* the flock of God that is your charge, not by constraint but willingly [as God would have you], not for shameful gain but eagerly, not as domineering over those in your charge but being examples to the flock. And when the *chief Shepherd* [Jesus Christ] is manifested you will obtain the unfading crown of glory" (1 Pet 5:2–4). The Letter of Saint

Paul to the Ephesians, in listing the offices that there are in the Church, explicitly mentions *pastors* (Eph 4:11), and the same Apostle sums up the attitude that those responsible for the Churches ought to have, saying to the presbyters of the Church of Ephesus:

> Take heed to yourselves and to all the *flock*, in which the Holy Spirit has made you overseers, [*to care for*; Douay-Rheims: *to rule*] to feed the church of the Lord which he obtained with his own blood. I know that after my departure fierce wolves will come in among you, not sparing the *flock*; and from among your own selves will arise men speaking perverse things, to draw away the disciples after them (Acts 20:28–30).

These priests whom Saint Paul counsels in pastoral terms are, in all probability, the pastors described in the Letter to the Ephesians.

By "pastoral ministry" in the Church is understood the totality of the activities carried out under the direction of the Pope and the bishops that are aimed at communicating the blessings of salvation. These activities are usually grouped as follows: (a) the ministry of the Word, (b) the ministry of liturgical worship, and (c) the ministry of leading, organizing, and directing the Church community. These subdivisions do not imply, however, that the three groups designated can be separated from one another, since these three sorts of ministry are, more precisely, different aspects of one sole ministry.

Since the revision of the Roman Missal after the Second Vatican Council, the saints who in this life were Popes, bishops, or priests are commemorated as "Holy Pastors". If we keep in mind the very rich meaning contained in the name of Pastor or Shepherd, as we have seen, we can understand the appropriateness of this terminology—and how stimulating it is for those who have been called to the sacred ministry.

The name of SHEPHERD or PASTOR is related to the names of BISHOP, APOSTLE, and PONTIFF or HIGH PRIEST.

SLAVE or SERVANT

"God, having raised up his Servant, sent him to you."

— ACTS 3:27

Slavery was a very familiar and widespread fact in antiquity. The lot of the servant or slave was quite harsh: the bottom line was a disregard for the right of every man to be free and not to be treated as the property of another man or as a beast of burden. A slave's fate depended, to a large extent, on the temperament and righteousness of his owner. The position of the slave was one of almost complete dependence upon his master. We should note that, between kindly masters and faithful servants, a relationship of affection and of reciprocal responsibility and loyalty would usually develop, a relationship that went far beyond the impersonal rights and duties established by law to regulate relations between masters and slaves. Scripture had advised the Israelites to show benevolence to their slaves, saying: "You shall remember that you were a slave in Egypt" (Deut 16:12), so that the memory of the hardships the Jewish people had suffered under Pharaoh's oppression (see Exodus, chapters 1 to 11) would serve to prevent them from doing the same thing to their slaves. This was an initial hint at what Jesus would say much later and in the broadest terms: "So whatever you wish that men would do to you, do so to them; for this is the law and the prophets" (Mt 7:12; see also Lk 6:27–38). At times, when one person wanted to address another with great respect, he would use the expression "I am your *servant*", or something similar (see, for example, 1 Sam 20:7; Josh 9:8).

The Jews had much more reason to acknowledge that they were servants of God: "For to me the people of Israel are *servants*, they are my *servants* whom I brought forth out of the land of Egypt: I am the LORD your God" (Lev 25:55). To recognize that one is a "servant of God" is a way of expressing one's total dependence upon God, an acknowledgement of his dominion and the willingness to obey him: exactly the opposite of the attitude of our first parents, when they sinned in paradise (see Gen 3:1–6). It is, therefore, a religious attitude, filled with love and not motivated solely by fear. When a man had been faithful to God, he would be called a "*servant of God*"; so it is said, for example, about Moses (Deut 34:5). It can be said that words such as those that young Samuel addressed to God: "Speak, Lord, for thy servant hears" (1 Sam 3:9, 10), summarize the entire religious disposition of a believer. To listen to God is to hear his word, to abide by it in faith, and to put it into practice. It is quite obvious, then, that the Virgin Mary, a faithful and pious daughter of Israel, as soon as she had learned of God's plans for her, concluded her dialogue with the angel by saying: "Behold, I am the *handmaid* of the Lord; let it be to me according to your word" (Lk 1:38).

We have already seen that in the book of the prophet Isaiah there is a poem of the "Servant of Yahweh" (Is 52:13— 53:12), which is reprinted in its entirety in the chapter that deals with the name of LAMB. That passage especially emphasizes the sufferings of the Savior of Israel and his humiliations, and it anticipates the other passage, this one in the New Testament, that gives Christ the name of Servant:

> Have this mind among yourselves, which was in Christ Jesus, who, though he was in the form of God, did not count equality with God a thing to be grasped [coveted], but emptied himself, taking the form of a *servant*, being born in the likeness of men. And being found in human form he

humbled himself and became obedient unto death, even death on a cross. Therefore God has highly exalted him and bestowed on him the name which is above every name, that at the name of Jesus every knee should bow, in heaven and on earth and under the earth, and every tongue confess that Jesus Christ is Lord, to the glory of God the Father (Phil 2:5–11).

In this passage from the Letter of Saint Paul to the Philippians, the name of servant is connected with obedience to the Father, and it has glorification as its consequence: a servant is one who obeys. Therefore this passage is explained by another, which discloses to us the sentiments of Christ upon entering this world, that is, when he became man in the womb of Mary:

Consequently, when Christ came into the world, he said, "Sacrifices and offerings thou hast not desired, but a body hast thou prepared for me; in burnt offerings and sin offerings thou hast taken no pleasure. Then I said, 'Lo, I have come to do thy will, O God'. . . ." And by that will we have been sanctified through the offering of the body of Jesus Christ once for all (Heb 10:5–7, 10).

Jesus himself said to his disciples, in reprimanding some of them for their desire to be great:

You know that the rulers of the Gentiles lord it over them, and their great men exercise authority over them. It shall not be so among you; but whoever would be great among you must be your *servant*, and whoever would be first among you must be your *slave*; even as the Son of man came *not to be served* but *to serve*, and to give his life as a ransom for many (Mt 20:25–28; Mk 10:42–45).

Here Jesus presents himself as a servant and notes precisely the meaning of his service: to give his life as a ransom for the redemption of many; this is the same meaning found in Isaiah 53:4ff., namely, to accomplish the salvific sacrifice of the

Cross. We must not forget that death by crucifixion was the way in which the Romans executed conquered peoples or slaves, and that is why the Letter to the Philippians underscores the paradox whereby Christ, in being put to death like a slave, received unsurpassable glory from his Father. In the Gospel of Saint Luke, as well, Jesus insists on the condition of being a servant: "For which is the greater, one who sits at table, or one who serves? Is it not the one who sits at table? But I am among you *as one who serves*" (Lk 22:27; verses 24–26 are parallel to Mt 20:25–28 and Mk 10:42–45).

In the Gospel, Jesus speaks in parables about *faithful and wise servants* (Mt 24:45) or about *good and faithful servants* (Mt 25:23) in referring to men who conscientiously carry out the mission they have received from God. Saint Paul (Rom 1:1; Tit 1:1), Saint Peter (2 Pet 1:1), Saint James (Jas 1:1), Saint Jude (Jude 1), and Timothy (Phil 1:1) give themselves the title of "*servants of Jesus Christ*". Saint Paul summarizes his apostolic outlook by saying: "I have made myself *a slave to all*, that I might win the more" (1 Cor 9:19) and "[we make] ourselves *your servants* for Jesus' sake" (2 Cor 4:5). When it is time to reward the diligent disciple, Jesus says to him, by means of the parable about the pounds [*minas*]: "Well done, *good servant*! Because you have been faithful in a very little, you shall have authority over ten cities" (Lk 19:17).

At a time when the bishop of Constantinople was attributing to himself a rather ambitious title, that of "Ecumenical" Patriarch (implying authority throughout the known world), Pope Saint Gregory the Great (in the late sixth and early seventh centuries), began to use the title of "*Servant of the servants of God*", and the Popes have continued to use it to this day.

The name of "servant", which belongs to Jesus, and which his Mother and the apostles used, provides an entire program of service and of humility that ought to be the distinguishing characteristic of the Church throughout the centuries, in fulfilling the word of God: "[L]earn from me; for I am gentle and lowly in heart" (Mt 11:29). If Moses, the mediator of the first covenant, "was very meek, more than all men that were on the face of the earth" (Num 12:3), and if the Mediator of the New Covenant, Jesus Christ, portrays himself as full of meekness, it is clear that one of the characteristics of the ministers of the Church has to be meekness. It is no mere coincidence that the word *minister*, which comes from Latin, and the word *deacon*, of Greek origin, both mean, literally, "servant".

The name of SERVANT has a special connection with the names of LAMB and SHEPHERD or PASTOR.

SON OF GOD

"You are the Christ, the son of the living God."

—MATTHEW 16:16

In the Old Testament, men, especially the Israelites, are occasionally called sons of God (Ps 29[28]:1 in the Hebrew; Is 30:1–9; 43:6; Hos 1:10), although in some cases this name serves as a bitter reproach: "A son honors his father, and a servant [fears] his master. If then I am a father, where is my honor? And if I am a master, where is my fear?" (Mal 1:6). In the New Testament, Christians are truly sons of God: "See what love the Father has given us, that we should be called children of God; and so we are" (1 Jn 3:1); this happens through the grace of baptism (see Jn 3:1–7).

> For all who are led by the Spirit of God are sons of God. For you did not receive the spirit of slavery to fall back into fear, but you have received the spirit of sonship. When we cry, "Abba! Father!" it is the Spirit himself bearing witness with our spirit that we are children of God, and if children, then heirs, heirs of God and fellow heirs with Christ, provided we suffer with him in order that we may also be glorified with him (Rom 8:14–17).

This state of being children of God has been produced by the coming of Christ.

> [W]hen the time had fully come, God sent forth his Son, born of woman, born under the law, to redeem those who were under the law, so that we might receive adoption as

124

sons. And because you are sons, God has sent the Spirit of his *Son* into our hearts, crying, "Abba! Father!" So through God you [being a Christian] are no longer a slave but a son, and if a son then an heir (Gal 4:4–7).

In the New Testament, the title of sons of God is given to the disciples of Christ much more frequently than it was used in reference to the Israelites in the Old Covenant (see Rom 5:2, Douay-Rheims; Rom 8:14–29; 9:8; 2 Cor 6:18; Eph 1:5; 4:13; Phil 2:15; Heb 12:7). The following passage emphasizes that our condition as sons of God depends on the sonship of Jesus: "For those whom he foreknew he also predestined to be conformed to the image of his *Son*, in order that he might be the *first-born among many brethren*" (Rom 8:29). In this sense, we are sons of God insofar as we are incorporated into Christ and are members of his Body, that is to say, united to him as the branches on the vine: in Christ we have been made "partakers of the divine nature" (2 Pet 1:4).

According to the words of David to his son Solomon, God had spoken to him about the latter, saying: "He [Solomon] shall build a house for my name. He shall be my son, and I will be his father, and I will establish his royal throne in Israel for ever" (1 Chron 22:10). With these words God had expressed his love for Solomon and his benevolence toward him; but we must keep in mind that Solomon was a prefiguration of Christ, in whom would be fulfilled abundantly the promises that were made to his ancestor. Only Christ would build the true house of God, which is the Church, and he alone is the king of the ages. The Psalms speak in a more explicit way about the Son of God:

> The kings of the earth set themselves,
>   and the rulers take counsel together,
>   against the LORD and his anointed [his Christ], saying,
> "Let us burst their bonds asunder,
>   and cast their cords from us."

> He who sits in the heavens laughs;
>   the LORD has them in derision.
> Then he will speak to them in his wrath,
>   and terrify them in his fury, saying,
> "I have set my king
>   on Zion, my holy hill."
> I will tell of the decree of the LORD:
> He said to me, "You are my *son*,
>   today I have begotten you.
> Ask of me, and I will make the nations your heritage,
>   and the ends of the earth your possession. . . ."
> Now therefore, O kings, be wise;
>   be warned, O rulers of the earth.
> Serve the LORD with fear,
>   with trembling.
>
> — Psalm 2:2–11

The Letter to the Hebrews (Heb 1:5) testifies to the messianic sense of the two preceding passages, as applied to Christ, so that their prophetic meaning is guaranteed by Sacred Scripture itself. The sense in which Christ is the Son of God is deeper than the sense in which we are sons of God, and, in a way, it is unique. Hence, the name of *Only-begotten*, which is given to him especially by Saint John: "[W]e saw his glory, the glory as it were of the *only begotten* of the Father" (Jn 1:14, Douay-Rheims); "No man hath seen God at any time: the *only begotten Son* who is in the bosom of the Father, he hath declared him" (Jn 1:18, Douay-Rheims); "By this hath the charity of God appeared towards us, because God hath sent his *only begotten Son* into the world, that we may live by him. In this is charity: not as though we had loved God, but because he hath first loved us, and sent his *Son* to be a propitiation for our sins" (1 Jn 4:9–10, Douay-Rheims). In the Gospel of Saint John, Jesus gives himself the name of Only-begotten Son during his conversation with Nicodemus:

For God so loved the world, as to give his *only begotten Son*: that whosoever believeth in him may not perish, but may have life everlasting. . . . He that believeth in him is not judged. But he that doth not believe is already judged: because he believeth not in the name of the *only begotten Son of God* (Jn 3:16, 18, Douay-Rheims).

That Jesus is the Son of God, son in a different sense than we are, is evident in the words he speaks to Mary Magdalene after his Resurrection: ". . . Go to my brethren and say to them, I am ascending to my Father and your Father, to my God and your God" (Jn 20:17).

Little by little, Jesus declared that he was the Only-begotten Son of the Father. When the Jews became indignant because he had cured a man on the sabbath, and they were persecuting Jesus because of it, he said to them: " 'My Father is working still, and I am working.' This was why the Jews sought all the more to kill him, because he not only broke the sabbath but also called God his Father, making himself equal with God" (Jn 5:16–18). Later on, again while disputing with the Jews, he said to them:

"Your father Abraham rejoiced that he was to see my day; he saw it and was glad." The Jews then said to him, "You are not yet fifty years old, and have you seen Abraham?" Jesus said to them, "Truly, truly, I say to you, before Abraham was, I am." So they took up stones to throw at him; but Jesus hid himself, and went out of the temple (Jn 8:56–59).

Soon afterward, Jesus told them in plain words:

"I and the Father are one." The Jews took up stones again to stone him. Jesus answered them, "I have shown you many good works from the Father; for which of these do you stone me?" The Jews answered him, "It is not for a good work that we stone you but for blasphemy; because you, *being a man, make yourself God*." Jesus answered them, "Is it not written in your law, 'I said, you are gods'? If he called them gods to whom the word of God came (and scripture cannot be broken), do you say of him whom the Father consecrated and sent into the world, 'You are blaspheming,' because I said, 'I am the *Son of God*'? If I am not doing the works of my Father, then do not believe me; but if I do them, even though you do not believe me, believe the works, that you may know and understand that the *Father* is in me and I am in the *Father*." Again they tried to arrest him . . . (Jn 10:30–39).

By this time, it was clear to the Jews that Jesus was proclaiming himself *the Son of God* in the sense that he was *equal to the Father*, one with him. They could not accept this because they took Jesus to be a mere man among many, and they did not know about the mystery of the Holy Trinity. When Jesus, glorified in his Resurrection, departs from this world, he gives a final and very important assignment to his apostles: "And Jesus came and said to them, 'All authority in heaven and on earth has been given to me. Go therefore and make disciples of all nations, baptizing them in the name of the *Father and of the Son and of the Holy Spirit*, teaching them to observe all that I have commanded you; and lo, I am with you always, to the close of the age'" (Mt 28:18–20). A little earlier, but still after the Resurrection, upon seeing the risen Christ, Thomas, the apostle who doubted, had exclaimed "My Lord and my God!" (Jn 20:28). Jesus did not correct this profession of faith but, rather, said to Thomas: "Have you believed because you have seen me? Blessed are those who have not seen and yet believe" (Jn 20:29).

In addition to this passage from the Gospel of Saint John, there is another New Testament passage in which the name of *God* is given to Jesus:

> For the grace of *God* has appeared for the salvation of all men, training us to renounce irreligion and worldly passions, and to live sober, upright, and godly lives in this world,

awaiting our blessed hope, the appearing of the glory of our great *God* and Savior Jesus Christ, who gave himself for us to redeem us from all iniquity and to purify for himself a people of his own who are zealous for [performing] good deeds (Tit 2:11–14).

It is interesting to note that, in the earliest Christian times, the condition for receiving baptism was to confess "that Jesus Christ is the *Son of God*" (Acts 8:37). Truly, the proclamation of the gift that God makes to us of his Son for our salvation (Acts 3 and 4; Rom 8:32ff.; 1 Cor 15:1ff., for example) is an essential part of the Christian message.

The name SON OF GOD is connected with the names of WORD, SON OF MAN, CHRIST, and JESUS. Although this name could have several meanings, in the Christian and Catholic faith, it means the second person of the Trinity, the Word who was made flesh in the womb of the Virgin Mary, who died for us, rose glorious from the dead, and who is One God with the Father and the Holy Spirit. In the New Testament, this name appears more than a hundred times.

SON OF MAN

"Hereafter you will see the Son of man seated at
the right hand of Power [of God], and coming on
the clouds of heaven."

— MATTHEW 26:64

The name SON OF MAN appears at least ninety times in the
New Testament. One could say that it is the name Jesus uses
most often in referring to himself.

The expression "son of man" occurs very frequently in the
Book of Ezekiel; God addresses the prophet by this name
(see, for example, Ezek 2:1, 3; 3:4, 10; 8:6, 8; 11:2, 15; 28:2,
12, 21; 32:2, 18). Here it simply means "man", perhaps also
with the connotation of being a member of the people of
Israel. Daniel, too, is called "son of man" (Dan 8:17) in the
same sense.

However, the use of this expression in the New Testament
has as a precedent a passage from Daniel that says:

> I saw in the night visions, and behold, with the clouds of
> heaven there came one like a *son of man*, and he came to the
> Ancient of Days and was presented before him. And to him
> was given dominion and glory and kingdom, that all peoples,
> nations, and languages should serve him; his dominion is an
> everlasting dominion, which shall not pass away, and his
> kingdom one that shall not be destroyed (Dan 7:13–14).

When Jesus was brought before the Jewish high priest
Caiaphas, the latter, trying to find a reason to condemn him,

asked him: " 'I adjure you by the living God, tell us if you are *the Christ, the Son of God.*' Jesus said to him, 'You have said so. But I tell you, hereafter you will see the *Son of man* seated at the right hand of Power, and coming on the clouds of heaven' " (Mt 26:63–64; Mk 14:61–62; Lk 22:67–69). Shortly before that, in the description of the Last Judgment, we read the following words spoken by Jesus: "When the *Son of man* comes in his glory, and all the angels with him, then he will sit on his glorious throne. Before him will be gathered all the nations, and he will separate them one from another. . . . Then the King will say to those at his right hand . . ." (Mt 25:31–34). The Book of Revelation says:

> Then I turned to see the voice that was speaking to me, and on turning I saw seven golden lampstands, and in the midst of the lampstands one like a *son of man,* clothed with a long robe and with a golden girdle round his breast; his head and his hair were white as white wool, white as snow; his eyes were like a flame of fire, his feet were like burnished bronze, refined as in a furnace, and his voice was like the sound of many waters. . . . When I saw him, I fell at his feet as though dead. But he laid his right hand upon me, saying, "Fear not, I am the first and the last, and the living one; I died, and behold I am alive for evermore, and I have the keys of Death and Hades" (Rev 1:12–18).

Again, in the Book of Revelation, this time in the context of a judgment, we read: "Then I looked, and lo, a white cloud, and seated on the cloud one like a *son of man,* with a golden crown on his head, and a sharp sickle in his hand" (Rev 14:14). To return to yet another passage from Daniel:

> I lifted up my eyes and looked, and behold, a man clothed in linen, whose loins were girded with gold of Uphaz. His body was like beryl, his face like the appearance of light-ning, his eyes like flaming torches, his arms and legs like the gleam of burnished bronze, and the sound of his words

like the noise of a multitude (Dan 10:5–6; probably this dignitary is the same one who is called "son of man" in verse 16).

If we read these biblical passages attentively, it is easy to see that they have elements in common by which they are interrelated: the name "Son of Man" is not simply synonymous with any human being but, rather, has connotations of glory, power, dominion, authority, and judgment. Although he is not identified with God, who is called "the Ancient of Days" or "the Father", he is very close to him and shares in his glory and power; yet this glory and this power are found in a being that has human traits. In light of the New Testament and the revelation of the mystery of the Holy Trinity, the image of the *Son of Man* approximates the title of "Son of God", and, in any case, means nearly the same as "the glorious Messiah", as is plainly evident in Jesus' reply to Caiaphas.

When Jesus refers to himself as the "Son of man", he does so in a wide variety of contexts. It can be to emphasize his *poverty and lowliness*: "Foxes have holes, and birds of the air have nests; but the *Son of man* has nowhere to lay his head" (Mt 8:20; Lk 9:58) or his attitude of *service*: "The *Son of man* came not to be served but to serve" (Mt 20:28; Mk 10:45). At other times, the context is the Parousia, or Second Coming of Christ: "Truly, I say to you, you will not have gone through all the towns of Israel, before the *Son of man* comes" (Mt 10:23); including the idea of *judgment*: "For the *Son of man* is to come with his angels in the glory of his Father, and then he will repay every man for what he has done" (Mt 16:27; 13:41; 19:28; Mk 8:38). The Son of Man is he who is to rise again (Mt 17:9) after being handed over by the Jews to be put to death (Mt 17:12; 20:18; 26:2, 24, 45; Mk 8:31; 9:31; 10:33; 14:21, 41; Lk 9:22). In some cases the title "Son of Man" is related to actions of Jesus that imply divine powers: " 'But that you may know that the *Son of man* has

authority on earth to forgive sins'—he said to the man who
was paralyzed—'I say to you, rise, take up your bed and go
home'" (Lk 5:24); or when he said to the Pharisees: "The
Son of man is Lord of the Sabbath" (Lk 6:5). But if we
compare the various passages in which this name is used, we
see that the connection with the glorious Second Coming
has special relevance:

> Then will appear the sign of the *Son of man* in heaven, and
> then all the tribes of the earth will mourn, and they will see
> the *Son of man* coming on the clouds of heaven with power
> and great glory; and he will send out his angels with a loud
> trumpet call, and they will gather his elect from the four
> winds, from one end of heaven to the other (Mt 24:30–31).

The name "Son of Man" is a messianic name, closely
connected with the Parousia or Second Coming of Christ in
his glory. Jesus prefers to use it when speaking of himself, and
there are two poles of meaning in this usage: the lowliness of
Jesus and, that notwithstanding, his dominion and glory. It is
related to the names of SERVANT, SON OF GOD, WORD, and
SPOUSE or BRIDEGROOM. In the sense in which Christ comes
into the world, it is related to another name that appears
several times in the New Testament: HE WHO IS TO COME.
"Are you *he who is to come*, or shall we look for another?"—
this is the question that John's disciples ask Jesus (Mt 11:3);
"This is indeed the prophet *who is to come* into the world!" (Jn
6:14). The early Christians lived their lives longing fervently
for the Second Coming of the Lord, and they frequently
repeated the prayer: "Come, Lord Jesus!" (Rev 22:17, 20;
1 Cor 16:22). The deacon Stephen sealed in this way his
profession of faith:

> He [Stephen], full of the Holy Spirit, gazed into heaven and
> saw the glory of God, and Jesus standing at the right hand of
> God; and he said, "Behold, I see the heavens opened, and the

Son of man standing at the right hand of God." But they [the Jews] cried out with a loud voice and stopped their ears and rushed together upon him. Then they cast him out of the city and stoned him (Acts 7:55–58).

Although "Son of Man" is a name hardly ever used in the Church today, except when it is read in the Scriptures, upon hearing it we ought to be inspired with that same longing which the early Christians had for the return of the Lord Jesus in glory and majesty to establish his kingdom at last, according to his promises.

SON OF MARY

"You will conceive in your womb and bear a son,
and you shall call his name Jesus."

— LUKE 1:31

The fact that Jesus is the son of Mary is declared many times in the Scriptures. Starting with the first announcement of the Savior: "I will put enmity between you [the devil] and the woman, and between your seed and her seed; he shall bruise your head, and you shall bruise his heel" (Gen 3:15) and continuing with the prophesy of Isaiah: "The Lord himself will give you a sign. Behold, a virgin shall conceive and bear a son, and shall call his name Immanu-el [= God-with-us]" (Is 7:14; see Mt 1:22), all the Gospels testify to this fact, so that Saint Paul can say: "[W]hen the time had fully come, God sent forth his *Son, born of woman*, born under the law, to redeem those who were under the law, so that we might receive adoption as sons" (Gal 4:4–5). In this way, the eternal Son of God, in taking on a true human nature in the womb of Mary, raises us, mere mortal men, to the status of sons of God: Mary is a very important part of this exchange in which God himself became man so that man might become God [see CCC 460].

Although Jesus was thought to be the son of Joseph, the husband of Mary (Lk 3:23; 4:22; Mt 13:55; Jn 1:45; 6:42), and although, in keeping with Jewish custom, his genealogy is recorded starting from or ending with Joseph (Lk 3:23–38; Mt 1:1–17), the Gospels clearly establish the fact that Joseph is not the natural father of Christ.

When *his mother* [that is, Jesus' Mother] Mary had been betrothed to Joseph, before they came together she was found to be with child of the Holy Spirit; and her husband Joseph, being a just man and unwilling to put her to shame, resolved to send her away. But as he considered this, behold, an angel of the Lord appeared to him in a dream, saying, "Joseph, son of David, do not fear to take Mary your wife, for that which is conceived in her is of the Holy Spirit; she will bear a son, and you shall call his name Jesus, for he will save his people from their sins" (Mt 1:18–21).

Saint Luke affirms the same thing:

And Mary said to the angel, "How shall this be [that I should become the mother of Jesus], since I have no husband [Douay-Rheims: I know not man]?" And the angel said to her, "The Holy Spirit will come upon you, and the power of the Most High will overshadow you; therefore *the child to be born* will be called holy, the Son of God (Lk 1:34–35).

Jesus, in his human nature, has no father; Saint Joseph is his foster father, the virginal spouse of Mary, who by the work of his hands provided for the Mother of God and her Divine Son.

The Gospels' insistence that Mary is the true Mother of Jesus (see, for example, Mt 1:16, 18, 24; 2:11, 13, 20–21; 12:46–47; 13:55; Mk 3:32; 6:3; Lk 1:26–38, 43; 2:3–7, 22–24, 33–34, 51; Jn 2:1–12; 19:25–27; Acts 1:14) is very important in establishing that Christ's humanity is genuine and not an illusion and that he is a member of the human race, true man, like us in all things except sin (2 Cor 5:21; Heb 4:15; 1 Pet 2:22). Furthermore, through Mary, the spouse of Joseph, Jesus is the *son of David* (Mt 1:1; Lk 1:32; 3:31), a name that is a messianic title well known to his contemporaries and used by them to refer to him or to address him: "Can this be the *Son of David*?" (Mt 12:23); "Have mercy on us, *Son of*

David!" (Mt 20:30–31; Mk 10:47–48; Lk 18:38–39). Jesus himself uses this messianic title to assert his divinity:

> Now while the Pharisees were gathered together, Jesus asked them a question, saying, "What do you think of the Christ? Whose son is he?" They said to him, "The son of David." He [Jesus] said to them, "How is it then that David, inspired by the [prophetic] Spirit, calls him Lord, saying, 'The Lord said to my Lord, Sit at my right hand, till I put thy enemies under thy feet' [Psalm 110:1]? If David thus calls him Lord, how is he *his son?*" And no one was able to answer him a word, nor from that day did any one dare to ask him any more questions (Mt 22:41–46; Mk 12:35–37; Lk 20:41–44).

When Jesus made his triumphal entrance into Jerusalem, he was acclaimed with this very name, Son of David:

> And the crowds that went before him and that followed him shouted, "Hosanna to the *Son of David!* Blessed is he who comes in the name of the Lord! Hosanna in the highest!" And when he entered Jerusalem, all the city was stirred, saying, "Who is this?" And the crowds said, "This is the prophet Jesus from Nazareth of Galilee" (Mt 21:9–11; Mk 11:9–10).

It is appropriate to recall Nathan's prophecy to David:

> "The LORD declares to you that the LORD will make you a house [dynasty]. When your days are fulfilled and you lie down with your fathers, I will raise up your offspring after you, who shall come forth from your body, and I will establish his kingdom. He shall build a house [temple] for my name, and I will establish the throne of his kingdom for ever. I will be his *father*, and he shall be my *son*. . . . And your house and your kingdom shall be made sure for ever before me; your throne shall be established for ever" (2 Sam 7:11–16).

It is evident that these words were not fulfilled in the kings who were descendants of David, nor in a political sense but, rather, in the Messiah King, as the multitude in Jerusalem acclaimed him, saying: "Blessed is the King who comes in the name of the Lord!" (Lk 19:38); although it is quite possible there were some people in the crowd who had messianic hopes that strongly emphasized the political aspect.

In the New Testament, there are several passages that speak of the "brothers" of Jesus (Mt 12:46–50; 13:55; Mk 3:31–35; 6:3; Lk 8:19–21; Jn 2:12; 7:3–5, 10; 20:17; Acts 1:14; 1 Cor 9:5; Gal 1:19). Many non-Catholic authors interpret these texts as though Mary had other children besides Jesus. The Catholic Church, from the most remote antiquity, has always professed the perpetual virginity of Mary, which means that Mary brought forth Jesus alone, who is called the "first-born son" (Lk 2:7) not because she then had other children but because he was the son consecrated to God, who had to be ransomed (Ex 13:12–15; 34:19–20; see the use of the term in Rom 8:29). Anyone who maintains that Mary had other children besides Jesus has abandoned the Catholic faith and the tradition of the ancient Church. This is why Catholic authors interpret these "brothers" of Jesus either as sons from a first marriage of Joseph, who would then have wedded the Virgin Mary in a second marriage, or else as cousins of Jesus, sons either of the Virgin Mary's sisters or of Joseph's brothers. A careful study of the texts in question does not favor the explanation involving a previous marriage of Saint Joseph.

For a Catholic, the fact that Jesus is the son of Mary is not something incidental; rather, it means that God has associated Mary in a certain way to his plan of salvation. The Church has regarded the words of Christ to his Mother, as she stood at the foot of the Cross: " 'Woman, behold, your son!' Then he said to the disciple [John], 'Behold, your mother!' " (Jn 19:26–27), as an expression of Mary's motherhood with respect to the Church. Mary is the mother of those who, having been incorporated into Christ, are made children of God by the redemption.

The name SON OF MARY is related to the name SON OF MAN and underscores our status as Christ's brethren (Jn 20:17) because of his true humanity and our adoption as sons.

TRUTH

"I am the Truth."

Truth is an attribute of God. "The ordinances of the Lord are *true*, and righteous altogether" (Ps 19:9); "a God of faithfulness and without iniquity" (Deut 32:4); "Thy faithfulness [extends] to the clouds" (Ps 36:5). That is why the believer adheres totally and absolutely to the word of God, because "the testimony of the Lord is sure . . ." (Ps 19:7). In Scripture, the theme of *truth* is, quite frequently, equivalent to that of *fidelity*.

The expression used by those sent by the Pharisees to Jesus, saying: "Teacher, we know that you are true, and teach the way of God *truthfully*" (Mt 22:16; Mk 12:14; Lk 20:21), even though their motive was hypocritical, expressed, nevertheless, something of which the people were convinced, since they considered Jesus to be a Teacher and Prophet: "You are right, Teacher; you have *truly* said . . ." (Mk 12:32).

At the beginning of the Gospel according to Saint John, we read: "And the Word became flesh and dwelt among us, full of grace and *truth*; we have beheld his glory, glory as of the only Son from the Father" (Jn 1:14), and a little further on, "[T]he law was given through Moses; grace and *truth* came through Jesus Christ" (v. 17). Jesus vigorously affirms that *his testimony is true* (Jn 8:14), that *his judgment is true* (v. 16), because "he [the Father] who sent me is *true*, and I declare to the world what I have heard from him" (v. 26). A very important passage follows: "Jesus then said to the Jews who had believed in him, 'If you continue in my word, you are truly my disciples, and *you will know the truth, and the truth will make you free*'" (vv. 31–32). The Jews, still preoccupied above all with temporal and political matters, answered him (with little regard for historical truth) that they had never been slaves to anyone (forgetting Egypt and Babylon), proud as they were to be descendants of Abraham (v. 33). Jesus, once again, made them see that the most profound problem with freedom was not found in the political order. "Truly, truly, I say to you, every one who commits sin is a slave to sin" (v. 34), and "if the Son makes you free, you will be free indeed" (v. 36). The truth that sets man free is the truth that convinces him that he is a sinner, that by himself he can do nothing to obtain salvation (Jn 15:5), and that only in Jesus Christ and through him do we have access to the Father through the forgiveness of our sins, which he merited upon the Cross. As long as man imagines that he is self-sufficient and believes that he can save himself, he will be in darkness, in error, and not in the truth, and he will not be able to give glory to God by acknowledging that "there is salvation in no one else, for there is no other name under heaven given among men by which we must be saved" (Acts 4:12), except by Jesus (see 1 Jn 1:8–10).

Jesus points out to the Jews the reason why they reject him:

"Why do you not understand what I say? It is because you cannot bear to hear my word. You are of your father the devil, and your will is to do your father's desires. He was a murderer from the beginning, and has nothing to do with the *truth*, because there is no *truth* in him. When he [the devil] lies, he speaks according to his own nature, for he is a liar and the father of lies. But, because *I tell the truth*, you do not believe me. Which of you convicts me of sin? If I tell the

truth, why do you not believe me? He who is of God hears
the words of God; the reason why you do not hear them is
that you are not of God" (Jn 8:43–47).

"You know . . . that no lie is of [comes from] the *truth*.
Who is the liar but he who denies that Jesus is the Christ?" (1
Jn 2:21–22). And "He who does not believe God has made
him a liar, because he has not believed in the testimony that
God has borne to his Son" (1 Jn 5:10), Jesus Christ. Just as the
tempter lied to our first parents in paradise, telling them that
if they disobeyed the command of the Lord they would
become like gods (Gen 3:1–5), and through their sin death
entered into the world (Rom 5:17ff.), so too, although "the
whole world is in the power of the evil one", we are of God,
and "we know that the Son of God has come and has given
us understanding, to know him who is *true*; and we are in him
who is *true*, in his Son Jesus Christ" (1 Jn 5:19–20). To believe
in Jesus Christ, who is the Truth, is to accept the fact that his
word is the supreme criterion by which to discern between
values and false values. And the fullness of truth consists of
the application of those values in everyday life, in every act of
our life, in every situation, in dealing with every man. The
most profound truth of man's being is for him to act in
complete conformity with God's designs. In that sense, truth
is a concept very close to that of salvation.

Jesus Christ is "the Holy One, the *True One*, who has the
key of David" (Rev 3:7); he is "the faithful and *true* witness"
(Rev 3:14), the one who has "come into the world, to bear
witness to the *truth*" (Jn 18:37).

The name of TRUTH is connected with the names of
WORD, WITNESS, LIGHT, PROPHET, and BREAD OF LIFE.

The Christian who seeks and cultivates the truth bears
witness to Christ; he who swears in the name of God in truth
honors the source of all truth.

VINE

"I am the true vine."

— JOHN 15:1, 5

The grapevine was a plant familiar to the Jews, so much so that they sometimes said that "every man sat under his vine" (1 Kings 4:25; Mic 4:4; 1 Mac 14:12). It was a symbol of fertility: "Your wife will be like a fruitful vine within your house" (Ps 128:3); "like a vine I caused loveliness to bud, and my blossoms became glorious and abundant fruit" (Sir 24:17). The absence of clusters of grapes on the vines and of figs on the fig trees is a symbol of Israel's misfortune (Jer 8:13). Israel's malice is compared to a desolate vineyard that is barren and shows no gratitude for the constant care of the vine-dresser, the Lord (Is 5:1–7).

Jesus develops this theme of the VINE in chapter 15 of the Gospel of Saint John. The point of the imagery is spiritual fruitfulness, the fruits that should be produced by those who are joined to the vine, and that only those who are united to Christ can produce. The key to the parable is simple enough: the Father in heaven is the owner of the vine and the vinedresser who looks after it (v. 1); Jesus is the vine, that is, the vine stock (vv. 1, 5); the disciples of Jesus are the branches (vv. 2, 4, 5, 6); the union of the branches with the vine stock symbolizes the union of the disciples with Christ (vv. 4–5); as the branch cannot bear fruit unless it is joined to the stock, neither can the disciple bear fruit unless he is united with Christ (vv. 4–5). The vinedresser prunes the branch that bears fruit so that it may give more fruit, and he cuts off the branch that does not bear fruit and throws it into the fire (vv. 2, 6); thus the disciple will be tested, and he who ultimately bears no fruit will be thrown into the eternal fire (see Mt 25:41ff.).

The passage is as follows:

> I am the true vine, and my Father is the vinedresser. Every branch of mine that bears no fruit, he takes away, and every branch that does bear fruit he prunes, that it may bear more fruit. You are already made clean by the word which I have spoken to you. Abide in me, and I in you. As the branch cannot bear fruit by itself, unless it abides in the vine, neither can you, unless you abide in me. I am the vine, you are the branches. He who abides in me, and I in him, he it is that bears much fruit, for apart from me you can do nothing. If a man does not abide in me, he is cast forth as a branch and withers; and the branches are gathered, thrown into the fire and burned. If you abide in me, and my words abide in you, ask whatever you will, and it shall be done for you. By this my Father is glorified, that you bear much fruit, and so prove to be my disciples (Jn 15:1–8).

The reading of this allegory of the Vine and the branches clearly implies that Christ is the origin of the new life that his disciples possess, a life led according to the Spirit that begins with baptism. This new life can be seen in the fruits of good works. The theme of the new birth to a new life is at the center of the conversation of Jesus with Nicodemus (Jn 3:1–21).

We should keep in mind that in this union with Christ, the origin of all spiritual fruitfulness, the word of God plays an important role: "You are already made clean by the word which I have spoken to you" (Jn 15:3); "if you abide in me, and my words abide in you . . ." (v. 7). Knowledge of Jesus through the gospel and of the salvific plan of God through the Sacred Scriptures is an illuminating grace that invites us to be identified with Christ. The word of God cleanses us from sin because it shows us that we are sinners and points the way to conversion. The words of Jesus abide in us; this is something that the Lord himself says in other, similar words: "If a man loves me, he will keep my word, and my Father will love him, and we will come to him and make our home with him" (Jn 14:23). Not to keep or heed the words of Jesus, which are the words of the Father, is a sign that we do not love him (v. 24).

This intimate union between the Lord and his disciples can become so profound that Saint Paul was able to say: "It is no longer I who live, but Christ who lives in me" (Gal 2:20).

The name of VINE that Jesus himself claims is very similar to that of HEAD: both emphasize that all LIFE that is lived according to God comes through Jesus. That is why Jesus' statement is categorical: "Apart from me you can do nothing" (Jn 15:5).

WAY

"I am the way."

This name, "the Way", that Jesus assigns to himself expresses the idea that we are going somewhere, toward something we have not yet reached: "[W]hile we are at home in [this mortal] body we are away from the Lord, for *we walk* by faith, not by sight. We are of good courage, and we would rather be away from the body and at home with the Lord" (2 Cor 5:6–8).

Referring to those whose hearts are hardened against the Lord, the Letter to the Hebrews says: "They always go astray in their hearts; they have not known my *ways*. As I swore in my wrath, 'They shall never enter my rest'" (Heb 3:10–11). Worse still is the case of those who were "speaking evil of the Way [of the Lord]" (Acts 19:9). One of the effects of sin upon men is that "the way of peace they know not" (Is 59:8), the peace of which Christ is the Prince (Is 9:6), "for he is our peace" (Eph 2:14).

With considerable hypocrisy the messengers from the Pharisees said to Jesus, "Teacher, we know that you are true, and teach the *way* of God truthfully, and care for no man; for you do not regard the position of men . . ." (Mt 22:16; Mk 12:14; Lk 20:21). The statement was true, but it concealed their ill will: they were trying to set a trap for him by asking him about the lawfulness of paying taxes to Caesar.

The passage in which Jesus gives himself the name of THE

WAY is clearly set in the context of our pilgrimage toward eternal life:

> "In my Father's house are many rooms; if it were not so, would I have told you that I go to prepare a place for you? And when I go and prepare a place for you, I will come again and will take you to myself, that where I am you may be also. And you know the *way* where I am going." Thomas said to him, "Lord, we do not know where you are going; how can we know the way?" Jesus said to him, "I am the *way*, and the truth, and the life (Jn 14:2–6).

These words of Christ are like an echo of the Psalm that says: "Teach me thy way, O LORD, that I may walk in thy truth" (Ps 86:11). Jesus is the way that leads to the Father, and it is to him that Saint Peter applies the words of the Psalm: "Thou hast made known to me the ways of life; thou wilt make me full of gladness with thy presence" (Acts 2:28; see Ps 16:11).

During the early years of the Church, and probably before the disciples of the Lord received or adopted the name of "Christians" (which happened for the first time in Antioch; see Acts 11:26), the new manner of living according to the gospel was called "the Way". "But Saul, still breathing threats and murder against the disciples of the Lord, went to the high priest and asked him for letters to the synagogues at Damascus, so that if he found any belonging to the *Way*, men or women, he might bring them bound to Jerusalem" (Acts 9:1– 2). In order to say that the governor Felix was acquainted with the doctrine Saint Paul was preaching, the author of the Acts of the Apostles notes that he had "a rather accurate knowledge of the Way" (Acts 24:22a). Using an equivalent expression that is a little more explicit, he speaks of the knowledge that Apollos had of Jesus: "Now a Jew named Apollos, a native of Alexandria, came to Ephesus. He was an eloquent man, well versed in the Scriptures. He had been instructed in the *way* of the Lord; and being fervent in spirit, he spoke and taught accurately the things concerning Jesus" (Acts 18:24–25).

The name THE WAY, which the Lord Jesus gives to himself, indicates that following him consists, above all, in identifying oneself with him who is the image of the invisible God (Col 1:15); those who are called to the faith must conform to him (see Rom 8:28–29), by the very fact that Christ is the firstborn among many brethren (v. 29). This is not to say that Christianity does away with the commandments of God's Law, since Jesus himself said: "If you would enter [eternal] life, keep the commandments" (Mt 19:17; Mk 10:19; Lk 18:20); instead, all the precepts of the Law acquire a new depth in Christ and make greater demands. Having established that the commandments are obligatory (see Mt 5:17–20), Jesus insists on their new dimensions: "You have heard that it was said to the men of old . . . but I say to you . . ." (Mt 5:21–22, 27–28, 31–32, 33–34, 38–39, 43–44). To say that Jesus is THE WAY is to say that he is the model for the lifestyle of the Christian, both in his relationship with God and also in his relation with his brothers. To say that Jesus is THE WAY is to underline the importance of contemplating him lovingly, so as to learn to be conformed to him.

The name THE WAY is connected with the names of MASTER, PROPHET, TRUTH, and LIGHT.

WITNESS

"Jesus Christ, the faithful witness."

— REVELATION 1:5

Only twice in the New Testament is Christ called by the name of WITNESS, and in both instances the word is qualified as "faithful" and "true" (Rev 1:5; 3:14). In the Old Testament, God calls himself by this name: "I am the one who knows [the judge], and I am witness, says the LORD" (Jer 29:23).

The essential quality of a witness is his truthfulness. In Sacred Scripture, false witnesses are severely reprimanded: "You shall not bear false witness against your neighbor" (Ex 20:16); "You shall not join hands with a wicked man to be a malicious witness" (Ex 23:1), because "a false witness will not go unpunished" (Prov 19:9), and "a false witness will perish" (Prov 21:28).

"God is true" (Jn 3:33; Rom 3:4), and Jesus Christ "is called Faithful and True" (Rev 19:11).

Whereas in the first three Gospels—of Saint Matthew, Saint Mark, and Saint Luke—the word *testimony* is used to refer to the witness men bear, sometimes falsely, against Jesus (for example, Mt 26:59; Mk 14:55–56; Lk 22:71), the Gospel of Saint John speaks repeatedly about Jesus as the one who gives testimony: "The world . . . hates me because I *testify* of it that its works are evil" (Jn 7:7). To the Jews who reproached him for giving testimony about himself, Jesus replied, saying: "Even if I do bear *witness* to myself, my *testimony* is true, for I know whence I have come and whither I am going, but you do not know whence I come or whither I am going. . . . I bear *witness* to myself, and the Father who sent me bears *witness* to me" (Jn 8:14, 18).

Jesus gives testimony that he is the Son of God, who has come into the world to save mankind. In order to be saved, men need to hold fast to the testimony of Jesus: to believe that Jesus Christ is the Son of God made man who offered his life on the Cross for our sins, and to receive his gospel, that is to say, the Truth, and to live according to it.

Before ascending to heaven, Jesus described the mission of his apostles in these words: "[Y]ou shall receive power when the Holy Spirit has come upon you; and you shall be my *witnesses* in Jerusalem and in all Judea and Samaria and to the end of the earth" (Acts 1:8). When the apostles decide to elect a disciple to replace Judas, Saint Peter says: "So one of the men who have accompanied us during all the time that the Lord Jesus went in and out among us, beginning from the baptism of John until the day when he was taken up from us—one of these men must become with us a *witness* to his resurrection" (Acts 1:21–22). The apostles present themselves as witnesses of Jesus (Acts 2:32; 3:15; 5:32):

> And we are *witnesses* to all that he [Jesus] did both in the country of the Jews and in Jerusalem. They put him to death by hanging him on a tree; but God raised him on the third day and made him manifest; not to all the people but to us who were chosen by God as *witnesses*, who ate and drank with him after he rose from the dead. And he commanded us to preach to the people, and to *testify* that he [Jesus Christ] is the one ordained by God to be judge of the living and the dead (Acts 10:39–42).

Saint Peter gives himself the title of "a witness of the suffer-ings of Christ" (1 Pet 5:1).

Those men and women who have given their life for the faith are witnesses of Christ in a very special way: "I saw under the altar the souls of those who had been slain for the word of God and for the *witness* they had borne" (Rev 6:9). The liturgy of the Church applies to them the title of "martyrs", a word of Greek origin that means, precisely, "witness".

The whole life of a Christian consists of giving witness to Christ, by one's faith and in one's works, and whether other men come to the faith and embrace the Gospel depends, according to God's plans, upon that testimony. Although all the sacraments of the Church give sanctifying grace to the one who receives them and impel him to give witness to Christ—"[T]hanks be to God, who in Christ always leads us in triumph, and through us spreads the fragrance of the knowledge of him everywhere; for we are the aroma of Christ to God . . ." (2 Cor 2:14–15)—nevertheless, one of them, the sacrament of confirmation, confers in a special way the power of the Holy Spirit to give good witness to the Lord Jesus. If the Christian does not give witness to Christ, this omission can cause those who do not know the Lord to reject him upon seeing the inconsistency of believers. "The name of God is blasphemed among the Gentiles because of you" (Rom 2:24). The Apostle Saint Paul himself, addressing Christian slaves, tells them: "Let all who are under the yoke of slavery regard their masters as worthy of all honor, so that the name of God and the teaching may not be defamed" (1 Tim 6:1).

The name of WITNESS is related to the names of TEACHER or MASTER, PROPHET, WORD, and TRUTH.

WORD OF GOD

"And the Word became flesh and dwelt among us."

— JOHN 1:14

The name of WORD has in common with the name of SON OF GOD that both express an intimate relationship with the Father, as well as the nature of that relationship, and not merely an office or an activity of Christ on behalf of mankind, as is the case with the majority of the names that Scripture attributes to him.

In the Old Testament, the concept of *Wisdom* is akin to the name of Word (see Wis 6:22—10:21). Wisdom appears in personified form (Prov 8:1—9:6) as a prediction of the revelation in the New Testament of the second Person of the Holy Trinity: the Word or Son of God:

> Ages ago I was set up, at the first, before the beginning of the earth. When there were no depths I was brought forth. . . . Before the mountains had been shaped, before the hills, I was brought forth. . . . When [God] established the heavens, I was there. . . . I was beside him, like a master workman; and I was daily his delight, rejoicing before him always. . . . For he who finds me finds life and obtains favor from the LORD (Prov 8:23–24, 25, 27, 30, 35).

Wisdom is God's design, prior to the creation of the world, but directed toward mankind: "[M]y delights were to be with the children of men" (Prov 8:31, Douay-Rheims). Making use of human concepts, we can say that the Word is the eternal Word spoken by the Father, one sole and complete Word, a Word that expresses him perfectly. But that Word is not merely a fleeting sound; rather, it is so full, powerful, and alive that it is a divine Person who has the same nature as the Father and the Holy Spirit.

That eternal Word, consubstantial with the Father, has manifested itself to mankind:

> In many and various ways God *spoke* of old to our fathers by the prophets, but in these last days he *has spoken* to us by a Son, whom he appointed the heir of all things, through whom also he created the world. He reflects the glory of God and bears the very stamp of his nature, upholding the universe by his *word of power*. When he had made purification for sins, he sat down at the right hand of the Majesty [of God] on high [= in heaven], having become as much superior to angels as the name he has obtained is more excellent than theirs (Heb 1:1–4).

The "word of power" that sustains all things is an expression that suggests the name of Word as Saint John describes it: "In the beginning was the *Word*, and the *Word* was with God, and the *Word* was God. He was in the beginning with God; all things were made through him, and without him was not anything made that was made" (Jn 1:1–3). It is very interesting to note so many similar features in the three biblical passages from the Book of Proverbs, the Letter to the Hebrews, and the Gospel of Saint John. The Book of Revelation speaks as follows:

> Then I saw heaven opened, and behold, a white horse! He who sat upon it is called Faithful and True, and in righteousness he judges and makes war. His eyes are like a flame of fire, and on his head are many diadems; and he has a name inscribed which no one knows but himself. He is clad in a robe dipped in blood, and the name by which he is called is *The Word of God* (Rev 19:11–13).

This Word of God is he who became man and dwelt among us, and "we have beheld his glory, glory as of the only Son from the Father . . . full of grace and truth" (Jn 1:14); these words of Saint John are the most explicit in identifying the Word of God with the Son of God; and so, just as the Son is One (the Only-begotten), so too the Word is one, because the eternal Word and Wisdom of the Father, which expresses his fullness, is unique.

The name of "Word" suggests both the communication within the Trinity and the will of God to communicate himself to mankind. Moreover, it is logical that that communication should be made by means of the Word, who is the eternal Word of God.

The words spoken by the Word are found in the Gospels. Gospel means "good tidings", "good news"; is this not an appropriate term to designate the book that contains the communication of the things of God? When the Father gave us his Son, his Word, he communicated to us all that he could communicate, all the intimacy of his being, all his loving plan of salvation. For this reason, the continuation of the work of salvation, which is entrusted to the Church, has as one of its chief elements the proclamation of the Gospel, or the ministry of the Word. When the word of God is proclaimed in the Church, it fulfills what Jesus said: "He who hears you hears me, and he who rejects you rejects me, and he who rejects me rejects him who sent me" (Lk 10:16). Hence, Saint Paul's insistence to his disciple Timothy:

> I charge you in the presence of God and of Christ Jesus who is to judge the living and the dead, and by his appearing and his kingdom: preach the word, be urgent in season and out of season, convince, rebuke, and exhort, be unfailing in patience and in teaching. For the time is coming when people will not endure sound teaching, but having itching ears they will accumulate for themselves teachers to suit their

own likings, and will turn away from listening to the truth and wander into myths (2 Tim 4:1–4).

The fruit of preaching is faith: "So faith comes from what is heard, and what is heard comes by the preaching of Christ [Douay-Rheims: by *the word of Christ*]" (Rom 10:17). The Apostle Paul desires that this word should "dwell in you richly, as you teach and admonish one another in all wisdom, and sing psalms and hymns and spiritual songs with thankfulness in your hearts to God" (Col 3:16). The power of the Word of God is emphasized by Saint James, as well: "Of his own will he brought us forth by the *word* of truth that we should be a kind of first fruits of his creatures" (Jas 1:18).

This is how Saint Paul describes his preaching:

> When I came to you, brethren, I did not come proclaiming to you the testimony of God in lofty words or [human] wisdom. For I decided to know nothing among you except Jesus Christ and him crucified. And I was with you in weakness and in much fear and trembling; and my speech and my message were not in plausible words of [human] wisdom, but in demonstration of the Spirit and of power, that your faith might not rest in the wisdom of men but in the power of God (1 Cor 2:1–5).

This power of God is so great that, as Saint Paul says, "most of the brethren [in Christ] have been made confident in the Lord because of my imprisonment, and are much more bold to speak the word of God without fear" (Phil 1:14), so that "the word of God is not fettered" (2 Tim 2:9).

In his First Letter to the Corinthians, Saint Paul sternly insists upon the respect due to the Body of Christ contained in the eucharistic Bread: "Whoever, therefore, eats the bread or drinks the cup of the Lord in an unworthy manner will be guilty of profaning the Body and Blood of the Lord" (1 Cor 11:27). In a similar way, the disciple of Christ must respect what has been spoken by the Word. A minister of the Church cannot preach his personal opinions as if they were God's words and, even less, demand the submission of faith to what is no more than an opinion, however respectable it may be, and not the word of God. To demand such submission would be to impose an odious tyranny, at the expense of the freedom of the sons of God. Nor is it lawful for a minister of the Word to abridge a reading, to omit systematically some teaching of the Lord, whether because it seems to be very demanding, or because the fear of men and human respect make it more convenient to keep silent about it. The Gospel must be proclaimed in all its purity, tactfully, and accompanied by the necessary instruction. And the disciple who listens knows that he is truly a disciple to the extent that he accepts the word and puts it into practice: "The seed is the *word* of God. . . . And as for that [which fell] in the good soil, they are those who, hearing the *word*, hold it fast in an honest and good heart, and bring forth fruit with patience" (Lk 8:11, 15; see Mt 13:23; Mk 4:14–20), in keeping with mission entrusted to them by Christ: "Go therefore and *make disciples* of all nations, baptizing them in the name of the Father and of the Son and of the Holy Spirit, teaching them to observe all that I have commanded you; and lo, I am with you always, to the close of the age" (Mt 28:19–20). This abiding presence of the Lord provides the power and the guarantee for the work of evangelization: he is in the Church through his Word, and the Church remains in him by hearing his Word: "If you abide in me, and *my words abide in you*, ask whatever you will, and it shall be done for you. By this my Father is glorified, that you bear much fruit, and so prove to be my disciples" (Jn 15:7–8).

The name WORD OF GOD is connected with the names of TRUTH, MASTER or TEACHER, BREAD OF LIFE, PROPHET, LIGHT, and WITNESS.

CONCLUSION

Saint Paul had no other purpose but to proclaim "the *unsearchable riches of Christ*, and to make all men see what is the plan of the mystery hidden for ages in God . . . that through the church the manifold wisdom of God might now be made known" (Eph 3:8–10). He wanted Christ to dwell in our hearts by faith, so that we, "being rooted and grounded in love, may have power to comprehend with all the saints what is *the breadth and length and height and depth*" of this mystery, "and to know the love of Christ which *surpasses knowledge*" so that we may be "filled with all the fulness of God" (Eph 3:17–19).

Something of that which continues and always will continue to be the task of a servant of God's Word is what this little book has attempted to accomplish—the product of some leisure time and relaxation during a vacation. The author asks forgiveness if something has been said incorrectly, or if something important has been left unsaid. Since his intention was to bring the reader closer to the Sacred Scriptures, much more can be found there (and better expressed) by anyone who wants to delve more deeply into the mystery of Christ by a study of his names, all of which are aspects of "the name which is above every name" (Phil 2:9). Each one of these names tells us something about the Lord Jesus, what he is or what he gives to us: something that we need. And therefore, in pronouncing that name, we could add each time, humbly and confidently: Have mercy on us! And let it be so.